Arizona's
Best Autumn Color

50 Great Hikes

TEXT AND PHOTOGRAPHY BY
Christine Maxa

www.westcliffepublishers.com

ISBN: 1-56579-424-9

TEXT AND PHOTOGRAPHY: Christine Maxa, © 2001. All rights reserved.
MAP ILLUSTRATIONS: Rebecca Finkel, © 2001. All rights reserved.

EDITOR: Kelly Kordes Anton
DESIGN AND PRODUCTION: Rebecca Finkel, F + P Graphic Design, Inc.; Fort Collins, CO
PRODUCTION MANAGER: Craig Keyzer

PUBLISHED BY: Westcliffe Publishers, Inc.
P.O. Box 1261
Englewood, CO 80150
WWW.WESTCLIFFEPUBLISHERS.COM

Printed in Hong Kong by H & Y Printing, Ltd.

LIBRARY OF CONGRESS CATALOGING-IN-PUBLICATION DATA:

Maxa, Christine.
   Arizona's best autumn color : 50 great hikes / text and photography by Christine Maxa.
       p. cm.
   Includes bibliographical references (p.).
   ISBN 1-56579-424-9
   1. Hiking--Arizona--Guidebooks. 2. Nature trails--Arizona--Guidebooks. 3. Arizona--Guidebooks. I. Title.

GV199.42.A6 M39 2001
917.904'54--dc21

2001026055

For more information about other fine books and calendars from Westcliffe Publishers, please contact your local bookstore, call us at 1-800-523-3692, write for our free color catalog, or visit us on the Web at www.westcliffepublishers.com.

COVER PHOTO: A collage of color in Coconino National Forest. Photo by Larry Ulrich.

PLEASE NOTE:
Risk is always a factor in backcountry and high-mountain travel. Many of the activities described in this book can be dangerous, especially when weather is adverse or unpredictable, and when unforeseen events or conditions create a hazardous situation. The author has done her best to provide the reader with accurate information about backcountry travel, as well as to point out some of its potential hazards. It is the responsibility of the users of this guide to learn the necessary skills for safe backcountry travel, and to exercise caution in potentially hazardous areas, especially on glaciers and avalanche-prone terrain. The author and publisher disclaim any liability for injury or other damage caused by backcountry traveling, mountain biking, or performing any other activity described in this book.

Acknowledgments

To my friends (Nance Coggeshall, Marty and Annette Cordano, Linda Welyk, Bruce and Mary Aiken, and Lisa Sharp), in all points of the state, who opened their homes and hearts while I hiked several days in their area: *Thank you!*

To my contacts at the managing agencies who double-checked my work and/or went the extra mile in obtaining answers to my questions: *Thank you!*

To Steve Yoder at the Arboretum in Flagstaff; Barbara Harris at the Coconino National Forest; Gregory F. Hansen, National Leave No Trace Program Coordinator at the USDA Forest Service; and the Desert Botanical Gardens Hot Line staff: *Thank you!*

This book is dedicated to Arizona Bob,
who said, "Christine, get a real job," and to
John Annerino, who said, "Christine, remember who you are."

A cascade down Wet Beaver Creek adjoining Bell Trail,
which winds its way to views of the Mogollon Rim.

Contents

Arizona's
Best Autumn Color
50 Great Hikes

Symbols in this legend are used in the maps for each hike.	
– – – Trail	Lake
----- Adjoining Trail	○ Point of Interest
—— Road	**TH** Trailhead
----- Dirt Road	**P** Parking
—— River	
35 Wildflower Hike	

Autumn Color Profiles

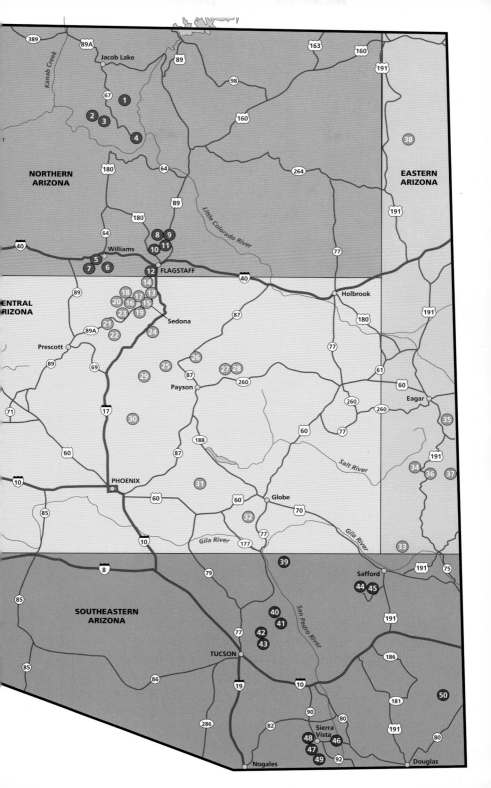

Introduction

There's something kinetic about standing in a forest in autumn. The mild fall air wraps its arms around you like an old friend, fallen leaves nudge you with their earthy pungency, and you're in a cocoon of color. Bigtooth maple trees flame red, become saturated in coral, or fluoresce orange. A yellow drape beams across a canyon wall from velvet ash, Arizona walnut, and boxelders. Leaves from Arizona sycamore trees sparkle like honey in the sun, their spicy sweetness filling the air. A forest of aspen illuminates a spruce-fir forest with a golden glow.

Like a scintillating show of fireworks in a black velvet sky, a rich display of fall color always elicits a response. From a pensive reflection to a verbal "wow," the experience is as soulful as the season it happens in.

On every trail I hiked for this book, autumn's color made a definite impression—from visual treats to reflective thoughts. Some trails, like colorful characters that blatantly grab your attention, made a dramatic visual impression that I can still conjure up in my mind. Other trails were akin to a lovely personality, with their unusual effects created by the colors, smells, and atmospheres. And a few trails were more moody and introspective, like the person you make surreptitious connections with and can never forget.

Many of the trails in this book are like old friends. I know them well and it feels good to be with them. But experiencing them in their fall attire often gave me a completely different impression and a new appreciation for them. Almost like hearing a friend from the office recite an original poem.

The way trees color themselves is interesting, too. In some tree communities, hundreds of trees are clonally connected by one rhizome, so they change colors in waves—aspens, for example. Others, such as maples, act like temperamental artists who won't perform except under ideal conditions. Some maples flushed entirely red, as if burning with embarrassment. Others in the same community either kept their summer green, preferring to wait awhile to color, or lit up like 40-foot torches—green on the bottom, yellow in the middle, and flame-red on top.

What this means is that trying to predict fall's moment of peak color enters a gambler's territory. Speculation makes the best call. The peak color times I have suggested for each hike are approximate, and can vary a week or two in either direction. Before setting out for a day of hiking, call the trail's managing agency for more succinct timing.

Happy hiking!

Opposite: *On the upper reaches of the Abineau–Bear Jaw Trail.*

How to Use This Guide

When planning your fall color hikes, go beyond considering the spots with the most spectacular photographs or the ones closest to your home. Consider the length and difficulty of the hike (see Appendix A for a list of trails arranged by difficulty). Each hike description includes a Trail Rating from easy to difficult. These ratings are defined as follows:

- **EASY** trails have well-marked paths and little or no grade, so almost anyone can do these hikes without difficulty.
- **MODERATE** trails are characterized by moderate grades and well-defined paths. Generally, some hiking experience is helpful in navigating these trails.
- **STRENUOUS** trails feature steep grades and generally well-marked paths, but are best suited to experienced hikers in good health.
- **DIFFICULT** trails have steep grades and/or challenging paths that may require route-finding skills. Difficult trails are only for experienced hikers in good health.

In addition to the Trail Rating, each hike description includes:

- **TRAIL LENGTH,** which you can often adjust by turning around sooner or walking farther
- **LOCATION,** such as a town, national park, or refuge
- **ELEVATION,** including loss or gain
- **CONTACT** name and phone number so you can check conditions
- **PEAK COLOR,** which can vary from year to year
- **SPECIAL CONSIDERATIONS,** which may include rules, fees, or trail advice
- **DIRECTIONS,** from a prominent town, landmark, or highway in the area

Again, I recommend that you review all these details before setting out on a hiking excursion. Trees and bushes that sport colorful foliage in autumn are set off in bold type in the book for easy identification. On some of the hikes, I mention that you may encounter black bears. Keep a safe distance to observe them. If you're concerned about the presence of bears, call the managing agency listed as the Contact for each hike before you set out on your trip. You can also follow these general principles: don't smell like food, don't run from a bear as it will think you are prey (plus, they can run and climb faster than any hiker), don't surprise a bear (create a little noise while hiking in bear country), and hike with others.

Opposite: *The Pumphouse Wash holds a rich collage of colors in a remote location.*

Leave No Trace

by Gregory F. Hansen, National Leave No Trace Program Coordinator, USDA Forest Service

The U.S. Forest Service introduced the idea of Leave No Trace in the 1970s, when the popularity of hiking and backpacking led millions of people out to enjoy their national forests and other public lands. This increased use brought about an overwhelming increase in human impact. Something had to be done to save these special places from literally being "loved to death." The Leave No Trace Program grew out of a need to teach the American people about minimum impact camping and to share with them an attitude of treading lightly on the land. The Leave No Trace concept is much more than just minimum impact camping—it is an awareness, an understanding, of our responsibility and connection to our natural environment.

The following seven principles will help you enjoy your outdoor experience in a way that leaves our public lands unimpaired for future generations. Visits to different environments—desert, mountain, seashore, wetland—each require different Leave No Trace methods. Make the effort to contact a local managing agency before each trip for information about the proper land ethics for that specific area. We can all help protect the natural integrity and value of our precious natural resources by working hard to Leave No Trace.

Leave No Trace Principles

PLAN AHEAD AND PREPARE. Proper trip planning and preparation—including obtaining information about geography and weather—help hikers accomplish trip goals safely and enjoyably while minimizing damage to natural and cultural resources.

TRAVEL AND CAMP ON DURABLE SURFACES. Damage to land occurs when visitors trample vegetation or communities of organisms beyond recovery. The resulting barren areas develop into undesirable soil erosion, trails, and campsites. When hiking, stay on the trail. If you must hike off trail, hike on the most durable surface (and if you're in a group, spread out).

DISPOSE OF WASTE PROPERLY (PACK IT IN, PACK IT OUT). Whatever you take into the backcountry, take out. Double-check your rest and lunch spots for anything left behind. To help prevent disease and contamination of water sources, dispose of human waste at least 200 feet from water, trails, and campsites (use a cat hole dug 6 to 8 inches deep).

LEAVE WHAT YOU FIND. Leave rocks, plants, animals, archaeological artifacts, and other objects as you find them. Examine—but do not touch—cultural or historical structures. This preserves the past and allows other hikers a sense of discovery.

MINIMIZE CAMPFIRE IMPACTS. If you must build a fire, the most important consideration is the potential for resource damage. Make a small fire using dead or downed wood. Whenever possible, use an existing campfire ring in a well-placed campsite. Skip the fire in areas where wood is scarce, such as in higher elevations, in heavily-used areas with limited wood supply, or in desert settings. Call the managing agency listed under Contact to inquire about fire restrictions; in some areas, campfires are prohibited.

RESPECT WILDLIFE. Quick movements and loud noises are stressful to animals. To avoid disturbing them, try to observe animals from afar. If your presence alters their normal activity, you are too close. Give animals a wide berth, especially during breeding, nesting, and birthing seasons.

BE CONSIDERATE OF OTHER VISITORS. While hiking, keep in mind:
- Travel in small groups.
- Keep noise level down. Let nature's sounds prevail.
- Wear clothing with colors that blend with the environment.
- Respect private property; leave gates the way you found them (opened or closed).

An old sawmill site along Miller Canyon Trail is surrounded by fall color beside the canyon's stream.

The Life Cycle of a Leaf

All trees have definite cycles of change and growth. While the changes in evergreens go unnoticed, deciduous trees show their internal transitions through the color, condition, and activity of their leaves.

In spring, buds that were lodged on twigs all winter wait for the precise time to start developing. The timing, which is in response to longer spans of daylight and warm weather, is so exact that all the trees in a particular area of a similar species often open their leaves on the same day. In general, a tree will open its leaves within a matter of hours of those in its community. However, variables such as the location of trees can interfere with the timing of leaf development.

The Bluff Loop trail drops down to Sabino Creek,
revealing the canyon's brightly-hued foliage.

As soon as the leaves unfold in the spring, they get to work supplying nutrition to the tree. This process is called photosynthesis, which literally means "putting together with light." The leaves produce food by combining the energy of the sun with carbon dioxide from the air and water from the soil.

The whole event takes place in cells located in the mesophyll layer (in the center of the leaf) in molecules of green pigment called chlorophyll. The chlorophyll absorbs sunlight and produces energy that combines with water and carbon dioxide to form glucose and oxygen. Glucose feeds the tree and oxygen supports other living creatures, humans included.

During the summer, leaves perform their daily task of producing glucose and distributing the sugar for immediate use through the trees' vascular system. Trees use the remaining glucose to produce buds, which will prevail through the upcoming winter, and to produce seeds.

By the end of summer, deciduous trees have completed their seed production and get ready to close down for the year. Since the creation of food requires water and sunlight, the shorter days and drier months of autumn have an effect on trees. The green chlorophyll starts to decrease and fade, and other colors start to appear.

Some of these other colors—pigments of carotenes and xanthophylls—reside in the leaf all year. As the chlorophyll decreases, the yellow color in trees increases.

A special process right inside the leaf forms red and purple colors. A combination of bright sunlight and cool nights precipitates a chemical process that creates anthocyanins—the pigments that turn leaves shades of red. At the beginning of fall, a layer of cells forms where each leaf stalk joins a branch. These cells block the flow of glucose from the leaf to the tree, but some is left behind. High sugar producers, such as maple trees, develop anthocyanin pigments (red and purple) from the sugar.

If leaves do not have enough sugar, the carotenoid pigments (orange) show through. If a frost occurs before the trees get a chance to create anthocyanins, the leaves will often brown out rather than change colors.

Colorful displays of fall leaves last a couple weeks before the leaves start to fall. Abscission causes autumn leaves to separate from their branches and fall to the ground. The abscission layer of cells, which cuts off the flow of glucose to the tree at the beginning of autumn, begins to dissolve, leaving only tiny vascular tubes to connect the leaf to the tree. Blustery fall winds or rainstorms batter the connections, and eventually they give way to release the leaves to the forest floor.

Once the leaves fall and carpet the forest floor, they continue to play a role in the environment as they decay and provide food for insects and nutrients for mushrooms and other plants.

North Kaibab Plateau: Arizona Trail

TRAIL RATING	moderate
TRAIL LENGTH	7 miles one way
LOCATION	Jacob Lake
ELEVATION	8,800–8,000 feet
CONTACT	Kaibab National Forest, 520-643-7395
PEAK COLOR	late September to early October
DIRECTIONS	From Jacob Lake, drive 24.8 miles south on Arizona 67 to FR 610 and turn left; after 1 mile the road forks. Take the left fork onto FR 611 and drive 4 miles to the trailhead.

This section of the near-complete Arizona Trail, which will stretch 790 miles from the northern edge of Arizona to its southernmost tip, was the first portion of the trail constructed from scratch. The trail travels through forests of mixed conifer and **aspen** trees separated by alpine meadows.

The route starts in a sun-drenched meadow that brings you to the rim of North Canyon after 0.1 mile. Once at the rim, you see a distant view of Marble Canyon, which shows up like a gash in the Colorado Plateau. You can spot dome-like Navajo Mountain and the rise of Utah's Kaiparowits Plateau along the northern horizon. **Aspen** trees gather just below the rim, beaming gold among the limestone cliffs.

Heading south and paralleling North Canyon, the trail enters a forest of mixed conifers drenched in pine sweetness. This moist and shady area harbors many wildflowers and bushes, the leaves of which may offer a bit of their own gold and reddish hues in the fall. **Aspen** stands often gather around the trail. **Creeping barberry,** mottled with scarlet, appear on the ground. **New Mexico locust** trees add bursts of yellow. At occasional breaks in the trees, you'll see the colorful red walls of North Canyon slicing through the cover of pine and **aspen** trees.

At about mile 1.5, the trail drops into a long meadow crowded with **aspen** trees along its borders. This meadow, and all the others along this trail, formed from a small valley. At night, cooler air settled in the valley, creating temperatures that were too cold for trees to survive. Consequently, the tree line edging the depression shows where temperatures remain more conducive to tree growth. You may spot a herd of mule deer grazing in these grassy meadows.

Near Crystal Spring, the trail joins FR 612A for almost 1 mile, then veers left off the road. The trail climbs out of the vale and over a ridge, then drops into another vale—a pattern the path repeats several times on the way to its end at the Grand Canyon National Park boundary. Blankets of strapping

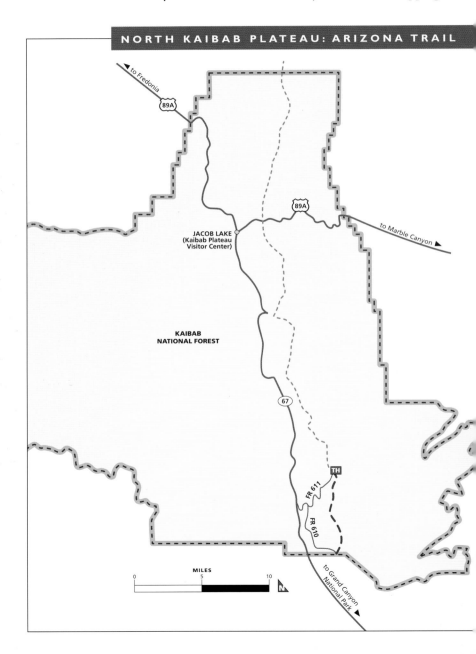

aspen trees often cover the ridges. On the hillside meadows, more mature **aspen** weave an exceptionally stunning pattern of gold among the dark firs.

Along the length of the trail, signposts displaying the Arizona Trail logo direct you. At times, wooden Forest Service signs may identify the trail as the Kaibab Rim Trail—same trail, different name. Simply follow the Arizona Trial signposts at all junctions. When you reach the national park boundary, return the way you came.

Aspen trees form a golden matrix within the dark green
of a coniferous forest on the North Kaibab Plateau.

Autumn
Hike 2

Fence Point:
Rainbow Rim Trail

Larry Ulrich

The 18-mile Rainbow Rim Trail traces the northern edge of the Grand Canyon, dipping into side canyons between five viewpoints that jut into the canyon like the fingers of a hand. The trail meanders through the Kaibab Plateau's common vegetation, which consists of **Gambel oak,** ponderosa pine, pockets of spruce and fir, and **aspen** trees. The deciduous trees produce stunning displays of color in the fall.

This section of the trail starts at the moody Fence Point viewpoint, located midway along the Rainbow Rim Trail, and heads north to Parissawampitts Point. The path enjoys the ruddy glow of the redwall formation within panoramic views of the Grand Canyon, but does so only briefly before it turns its back on the chasm and cuts across the peninsula of the plateau toward Parissawampitts Canyon. The path weaves in and out of the russet and golden cover of **Gambel oak** groves, the trees' spindly trunks leaning every which way. Colonies of **creeping barberry** paint scarlet trails along the ground. At mile 2, you'll see

TRAIL RATING moderate

TRAIL LENGTH up to 5.5 miles one way

LOCATION North Rim of the Grand Canyon

ELEVATION 7,550–7,350 feet

CONTACT Kaibab National Forest, 520-643-7395

PEAK COLOR end of September to beginning of October

DIRECTIONS From Jacob Lake, drive 26.5 miles south on Arizona 67 and turn right on FR 22 at DeMotte Park. After about 10 miles you will reach FR 206. Turn south (left) onto FR 206 and drive about 8 miles to FR 293. Turn right and drive west on FR 293 for about 8 miles to the trailhead.

FENCE POINT: RAINBOW RIM TRAIL

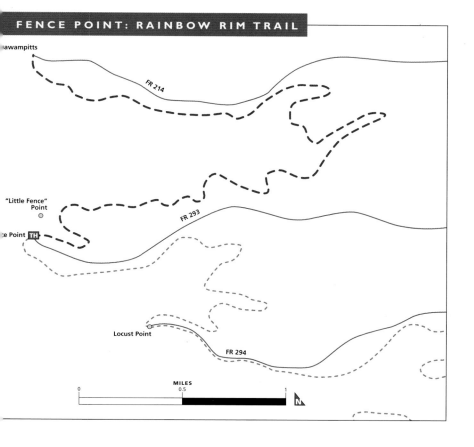

the gold of **aspen** leaves in Parissawampitts Canyon. The **aspen** trees grow so thick that the canyon seems to glow gold.

Parissawampitts Spring, tucked deeply into the side canyon, provides a moist environment that coaxes **aspen** trees to proliferate. The canyon's name derives from the Paiute Indian word "parush," meaning flowing water.

The trail parallels Parissawampitts Canyon for 0.5 mile before it starts to descend into the yellow glow. Watch for dabs of red and gold color on wild geranium colonies as the trail drops into the canyon. The intense fall color carries on for about 1 mile, during which time the trail crosses the canyon and continues up its other side, where you can view the color from the south face of the canyon.

When the trail reaches the rim and pulls away from the canyon, the color stops abruptly. Then, in another 0.25 mile, the fall color performs an encore at a drainage just west of the trail filled with **aspen** and **Gambel oak** trees. As long as the trail parallels this canyon (for about 1 mile), you'll see color. When the color stops completely, you can return the way you came or continue another 1.5 miles to the Parissawampitts Point Trailhead.

North Timp Point: Rainbow Rim Trail

Larry Ulrich

TRAIL RATING moderate

TRAIL LENGTH 3.5–6.5 miles one way

LOCATION North Rim of the Grand Canyon

ELEVATION 7,600 feet

CONTACT Kaibab National Forest, 520-643-7395

PEAK COLOR end of September to beginning of October

DIRECTIONS From Jacob Lake, drive 26.5 miles south on Arizona 67 and turn right on FR 22 at DeMotte Park. After about 10 miles you will reach FR 206. Turn south (left) onto FR 206 and drive about 11 miles to FR 271. Turn right and drive west about 5 miles to the fork in the road. Take a right onto FR 271A and drive 3 miles to the trailhead.

This section of the 18-mile Rainbow Rim Trail starts at North Timp Point, the second of the trail's five viewpoints located along the Grand Canyon's north rim. North Timp Point is the only easily accessible point on the North Kaibab where you can glimpse Thunder River gushing from the north wall of Tapeats Canyon.

The trail edges the North Timp Point peninsula, dips into a side canyon called Timp Canyon, then climbs out of Timp Canyon to another viewpoint called Locust Point. The true beauty of this trail lies in the scenic views of the Grand Canyon—which you get to enjoy for free—displayed along it.

As the trail heads north around North Timp Point, you get a look at the Grand Canyon's unique formations of Kaibab limestone along the canyon's rim. **Gambel oak** trees add a russet color, and **creeping barberry** blush red in the first 0.5 mile. Then, the trail pulls away from the canyon and heads into ponderosa pine parks. By mile 1, you'll see golden **aspen** leaves glittering in the wind.

During the next 3 miles, pockets of **aspen** appear often as the trail winds through the ponderosa pine parks. Some are buried deep in the pines, while others crowd around the trail. By mile 2, you're never far from glints of gold.

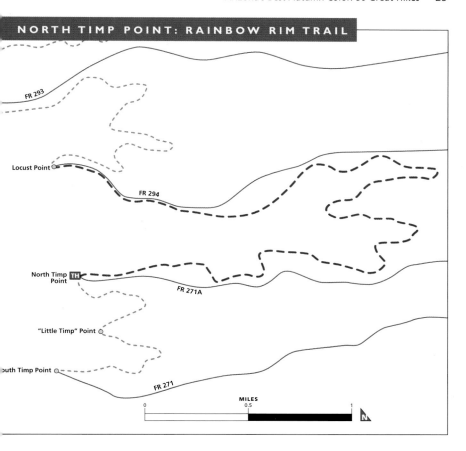

NORTH TIMP POINT: RAINBOW RIM TRAIL

FR 293

Locust Point

FR 294

North Timp Point **TH**

FR 271A

"Little Timp" Point

South Timp Point

FR 271

MILES
0   0.5   1

At mile 3, the trail enters a particularly nice section, zigzagging into Timp Canyon through a gathering of pine, **aspen**, and spruce trees. The trail eventually lands in a grassy meadow with clusters of **aspen**, then climbs back onto the Kaibab Plateau. At this point, fall colors become sparse, but you may want to continue 3 more miles to Locust Point, the next viewpoint along the trail. If not, return the way you came.

North Kaibab Trail

TRAIL RATING	strenuous
TRAIL LENGTH	2.7–4.7 miles one way
LOCATION	North Rim of the Grand Canyon
ELEVATION	8,250–5,200 feet
CONTACT	Grand Canyon National Park, 520-638-7888
PEAK COLOR	early October
SPECIAL CONSIDERATIONS	The national park charges a $20 entrance fee per car.
DIRECTIONS	From Jacob Lake, drive south on Arizona 67 about 30 miles to Grand Canyon National Park's North Rim entrance gate. Go 11 miles to the trailhead on the east (left) side of the road.

As one of Grand Canyon National Park's "corridor trails," the North Kaibab Trail gets regular maintenance from park service employees, who remove rock avalanches and washouts that add challenges to unmaintained trails. The only problem you might encounter on this trail is the climb out—which is really something to consider, as the return hike on this section of the trail requires you to climb up to 3,000 feet.

The trail drops through about nine different geological formations in Roaring Springs Canyon on its way to its confluence with Bright Angel Canyon at Roaring Springs. Along the way, it passes several sources of fall color, including **aspen, bigtooth** and **Rocky Mountain maple, Gambel oak, boxelder,** and **Fremont cottonwood** trees.

The route starts in **aspen** country, which assumes its fall glow in early October. The **aspen** trees follow the trail for about 0.5 mile into the Toroweap formation, where **bigtooth maple, Gambel oak,** and **Rocky Mountain maple** trees begin to pour over the trail to form a colorful corridor of yellows, oranges, and reds. During the first mile, the trail passes a couple overlooks that give you a chance to see the patchwork of color down the sides of the canyon walls. The overlooks will also help you catch your breath on the climb out.

Maple and **Gambel oak** trees proliferate on the trail's drop through the ruddy Hermit Shale formation. Watch for **creeping barberry** coloring the edges of the trail. By the time you get to the Supai Tunnel, at mile 2.7, the hardwood color slows down noticeably.

If you decide to continue the hike to Roaring Springs, the yellow and russet meld of color from the **Gambel oak** trees prevails as the trail leaves the **maples** behind. However, when the trail crosses the canyon or passes feeder drainages, look for **boxelder, Fremont cottonwood,** and occasional **bigtooth maple** trees that congregate in these moist areas. The last of the **bigtooth maple** trees appear at a pour off just before the Roaring Spring pump house.

If you hike to the pump house, continue 0.25 mile to the pump house residence where Bruce and Mary Aiken live. Besides operating the flow of

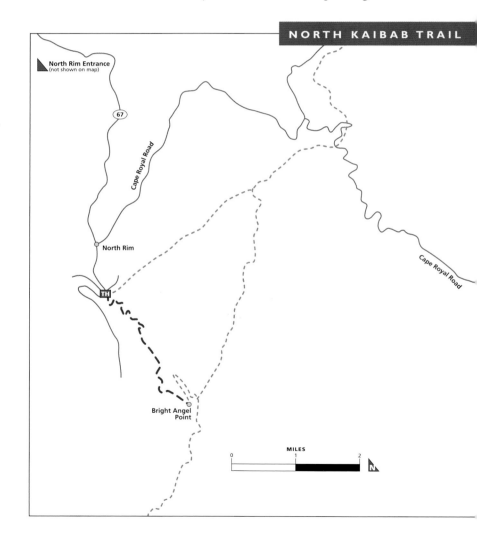

water from the pump house to the national park, Bruce Aiken is a world-class Grand Canyon artist. The Aikens will provide interesting conversation and the occasional glass of electrolyte-fortified lemonade to refresh corridor trail hikers.

ASPEN
Populus tremuloides

Aspens play an important role in the ecology of the forest. Also called "mothers of the forest," aspen create a nurturing environment in which conifers can thrive. Because of this, the aspen are dependent on fire to continue their perpetual life cycles.

After a fire in a conifer forest, aspen seeds or suckers from existing root systems will sprout in the land cleared by the flames. After a decade or two, the aspens' shade creates a cool and moist environment for conifers to spring up. By the time the aspens have lived a century, the conifers have grown to the same height, and the trees compete for sunshine. In another 50 years, however, the conifers usually win, growing taller than the aspen. The aspen die out, leaving decayed trunks that make temporary homes for fungus and insects before they dissolve and return nutrients to the soil.

When another fires levels the conifer forest, the aspen life cycle begins again.

With their silver-white trunks and clattering bright yellow leaves, aspen create dramatic fall displays. The leaves quiver from the slightest breezes because they have flat stems attached perpendicularly to their surface.

Each stand of aspen often seems to take on its own hue of gold. This phenomenon, called clonal growth, happens when the trees are all related (growing off one root rhizome). A thousand aspen trees can be connected to one rhizome. Closely spaced and similar in height, the clonal trees have the same type of bark and stature, and they lose their leaves at the same time.

*Autumn
Hike 5* *Bill Williams Trail*

TRAIL RATING	strenuous
TRAIL LENGTH	4 miles one way
LOCATION	Williams
ELEVATION	7,000–9,256 feet
CONTACT	Kaibab National Forest, 520-635-2676
PEAK COLOR	early October
SPECIAL CONSIDERATIONS	Motorized vehicles are prohibited on the trail.
DIRECTIONS	From Interstate 40 in Williams, take Exit 161 (Arizona 64) and turn southwest (right) onto Clover Hill Road (frontage road). Go to the Williams District Ranger Station and follow the signs to the trailhead.

Once a toll road built in 1902, the Bill Williams Trail provides the shortest route to the top of its namesake mountain. Bill Williams Mountain, named after the rugged mountain man who hung out in Arizona's wild backcountry in the mid-1800s, is the area's tallest mountain. Williams was the area's most colorful mountain man.

Williams, with his eccentric personality and cold demeanor, was known as Old Solitaire. He took to the backcountry after almost a decade of transient preaching. A wiry redhead known for drunkenness, Williams handled a rifle like a sharpshooter and navigated through Indian territory like a scout. Another mountain man, Anton Leroux, named the mountain for Williams two years after a war party of Ute Indians killed him.

Heading south, the trail's 2,300-foot climb starts out slowly in a loose-knit forest of mixed conifers strewn with volcanic rocks and boulders. At the intersection with the Clover Spring Trail, only a short distance from the trailhead, the path levels off a bit before it starts to climb again at mile 1. By that time, **Gambel oak** trees toss in their gold and russet colors along the trail, while surrounding slopes show off hues of yellow, gold, and orange.

The trail enjoys a moderate pitch as it makes its steady climb up the mountain. By mile 2, you'll start to see **aspen** trees growing in the West Cataract Creek drainage to the west of the trail. As the drainage rises to meet the trail, the fall color joins the path. Just beyond mile 2, **New Mexico locust** trees gather along the drainage, making the route exceptionally bright with their yellow glow. When the creek crosses the trail, **Rocky Mountain maple** trees gather around it and add reddish hues.

During the last mile, as the trail climbs more steeply deep in the **aspen**-fir forest, you'll see several rock formations that rise from the forest floor matching the charcoal-gray boulders strewn along the trail. **Gooseberry** bushes add splashes of yellow along the trail, and **creeping barberry** add dashes of scarlet.

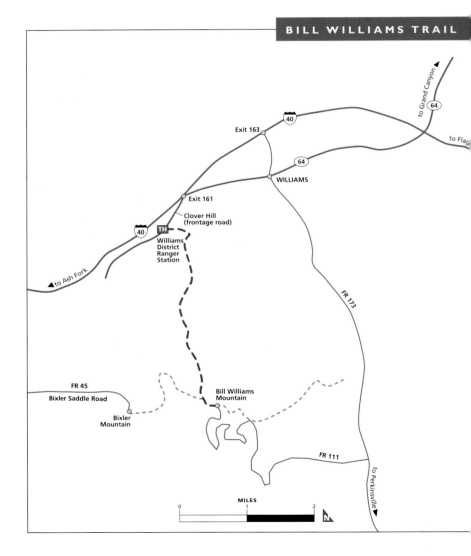

When the trail intersects FR 111, split log benches offer a place to rest. After crossing the road, the trail passes through a small meadow fringed with **aspen** trees, then finishes the last 0.5 mile on the road, which winds up to the top of the mountain. Along the way, the trail shows off panoramic views of the Colorado Plateau stretching to the west of the mountain. Once on top of the mountain, you can see the Bill Williams Lookout Tower surrounded by stands of **aspen**. Return the way you came.

GAMBEL OAK
Quercus gambelii

Gambel oak trees like to mingle with mixed conifers and ponderosa pines, where they can reach tree size. In canyons, Gambel oak trees often form strapping thickets.

The leaves of Gambel oak range in color from gold to reddish russet in the fall. Often, the leaves do not drop from the branches during winter, but remain to clatter in the wind.

Many bygone cultures associated oak trees with thunder gods. Zeus, one of the Greek gods, considered the oak a sacred tree, and Europeans associated it with their thunder god, Thor. The thunder god tie-in may originate from the trees' propensity to attract lightning. The Navajos used lightning-struck oaks for certain implements in ceremonies.

*Autumn
Hike 6* Benham Trail

TRAIL RATING	strenuous
TRAIL LENGTH	4.5 miles one way
LOCATION	Williams
ELEVATION	7,270–9,256 feet
CONTACT	Kaibab National Forest, 520-635-2676
PEAK COLOR	early October
DIRECTIONS	From Interstate 40, take Exit 163 south to Williams. From Williams, go south on Fourth Street (FR 173) for about 3.5 miles and take a sharp right (on unmarked FR 140), following signs to the trailhead.

The Forest Service built the Benham Trail in 1920 to create a moderate route up to the top of Bill Williams Mountain. Named for Ranger H.L. Benham, the trail leads to the lookout tower atop the mountain. Since 1905, the Forest Service has used a lookout tree, and later a lookout tower, to spot forest fires on this mountain.

The trail starts in a forest of ponderosa pines with a scattering of **Gambel oak** trees that add golden glimmers. Looking up the mountain from the trailhead, you'll see a checkerboard of color created by a meld of **aspen, Gambel oak,** and mixed conifer trees. The climb up the mountain starts gradually. As the trail gains in elevation, fir trees add to the evergreen mix, and **Gambel oak** trees gather thickly. Occasional clearings allow glimpses of the gold and russet colors blanketing neighboring slopes.

By mile 2, after the trail crosses FR 111, the grade becomes more serious. Fir trees become more abundant and **New Mexico locust** trees add more gold color. More views of surrounding peaks topped with color peek through as well. The trail makes another road crossing, then enters into a stand of **aspen** as it zigzags farther up the mountain.

After the third road crossing, the trail enters a meadow, then eventually takes to the road for the last 0.5 mile. FR 111 takes you all the way to the top of the mountain, which the Havasupai Indians called Bear Mountain. The

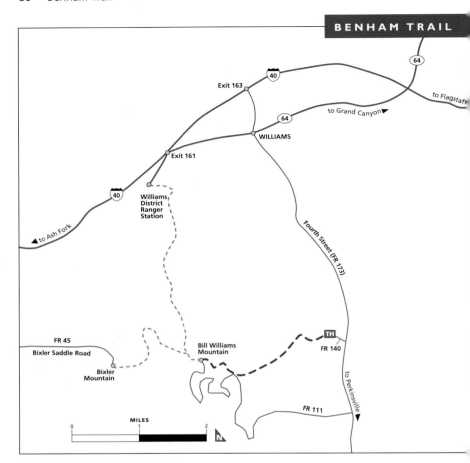

gooseberry and wild raspberry bushes lining the road provide juicy bear meals in the summer and add a yellow glow to the fir and aspen mix when their leaves turn color in the fall. Aspen trees gather around the top where the Bill Williams Lookout Tower stands. A red outhouse, dated but useful, adds its own colorful touch. Return the way you came.

Bixler Saddle Trail

TRAIL RATING	moderate
TRAIL LENGTH	2—2.5 miles one way
LOCATION	Williams
ELEVATION	7,700—8,740 feet
CONTACT	Kaibab National Forest, 520-635-2676
PEAK COLOR	early October
DIRECTIONS	From Interstate 40, take Exit 157 and go south on Williams Loop Road (FR 108) for about 1 mile. Turn east (left) onto Bixler Saddle Road (FR 45) and drive 3.1 miles to the trailhead. Bixler Saddle Road is a high-clearance road.

The Bixler Saddle Trail, named for a rancher in the area, starts on the saddle between Bixler and Bill Williams Mountains. Large cairns mark the trail's route as it makes a steadily steep climb up the western slope of the double-peaked, lava-cone formation of Bill Williams Mountain. Lava cobbles, remnants of ancient volcanism that formed the area's mountains, cover the trail. Attractive volcanic formations rise on either side of the path.

Thick groves of **Gambel oak** trees surround the trail on its initial climb up the mountain. In 0.5 mile, the trail becomes noticeably steeper as it cuts through a stand of **aspen** trees. With **Gambel oak** trees on one side and **aspen**

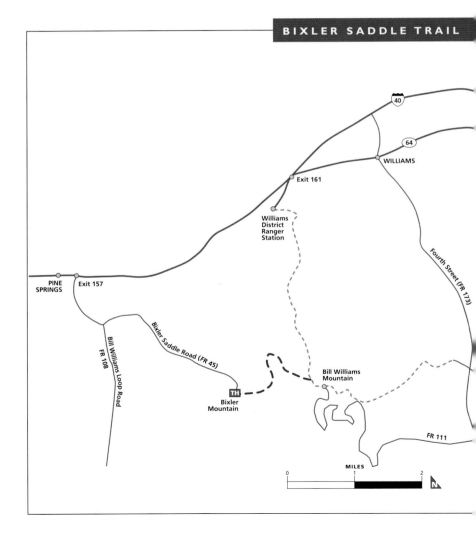

BIXLER SADDLE TRAIL

trees on the other, the trail settles down again. Here, a break in the trees shows off the blanket of color on the slope of Bill Williams Mountain and neighboring slopes to the south.

A little farther along, the trail contours the edge of the mountain. The trees open up a window to a western panorama of the Colorado Plateau. The trail then dips back into the forest and continues its route along the edge of the mountain. Through the trees, you'll still catch glimpses of peaks colored with fall foliage on distant ridges.

The trail breaks free from the forest and zigzags up to an exposed saddle. On the saddle, you get a view of a ring of peaks circling the mountain, each one distinctive in shape and streaked with fall color. You may also notice a line of white rocks along a clearing on the saddle. The rocks outline a landing area for helicopters used in fire suppression.

The last 0.5 mile heads east and passes through a colorful spread of **Gambel oak** trees. Just before the trail crosses another saddle and reaches the end at its junction with the Bill Williams Trail, the oaks evanesce.

At the saddle, you get a view of the golden matrix of **aspen** trees in the dark firs draping the mountaintops. The trail heads into the mixed conifer and **aspen** forest where the Bill Williams Trail continues to climb to the top of the mountain. Return the way you came, or continue another 0.5 mile to the end of the Bill Williams Trail.

Abineau–Bear Jaw Loop

TRAIL RATING	difficult
TRAIL LENGTH	7-mile loop
LOCATION	Flagstaff
ELEVATION	8,500–10,400 feet
CONTACT	Coconino National Forest, 520-526-0866
PEAK COLOR	late September to early October
DIRECTIONS	From Flagstaff, drive north on US 89 about 17 miles. Turn west (left) onto FR 552 (about 1 mile north of the Sunset Crater turnoff). Drive 1 mile to FR 418 and turn north (right). Go 7.6 miles to FR 9123J and turn south (left). Drive 0.7 mile to the trailhead.

When they think about aspen leaves in the fall, most Arizonans automatically think gold. But some **aspens** add a red blush to their golden glow, which produces a striking display of color. The red comes from the genetic makeup of the trees. Some biologists attribute the red to a microclimate adaptation where the trees are exposed to sudden freezes; others think it's a clonal mutation. About midway along this loop hike, where the **aspen** trees gather so thickly they seem to illuminate the mountain slopes, you'll see this phenomenon.

Situated on the less-visited north face of the San Francisco Peaks, the trail starts off in a pine meadow on an old road that starts from the parking lot. The route continues onto a single track that veers right through a mixed conifer and **aspen** forest. At mile 0.5, a sign directs you to turn right for the Abineau Trail and left for the Bear Jaw Trail.

The Abineau Trail begins a steep climb up the backside of the mountain in Abineau Canyon. The thick stands of mixed conifers stuffed inside the narrow canyon give it a dark, mysterious feel, but the trail often gets a bright dose of gold from frequent stands of **aspen**. The dark earthen path, scattered with pinecones and charcoal-gray lava cobbles, features dabs of scarlet from the colonies of **creeping barberry** trailing next to it.

At about mile 1.25, the canyon opens up and parts the forest, allowing views of Mt. Humphreys brooding above. Sun-drenched and boulder strewn, the trail rubs shoulders with a drainage that accommodates snowmelt from Arizona's highest peak as it climbs past **gooseberry** bushes and **baneberry** plants that add splashes of yellow. In this subalpine region, the landscape becomes ragged with dry fall from the intense weather conditions that tear at the trees.

The trail takes its time, scrambling over boulders as it momentarily becomes one with the drainage, then finally climbing to the west side. Take a look at the panorama behind you to the north, where volcanic cones swell out of the Colorado Plateau and the north rim of the Grand Canyon rises on the horizon. After a short distance, the trail crosses the drainage one more time and, by mile 1.5, joins up with an old road that eventually connects it to the Bear Jaw Trail. From here on, the route is all downhill.

The old road cuts through a thick cover of mixed conifers flecked with gold from the occasional **aspen** tree. After about 1 mile, the road descends into a large stand of **aspen**. At each turn in the road, you'll see thick cloaks of gold draping the surrounding slopes. Here is where you notice the red-leaved **aspen** trees. In another mile, you come to the signed junction with the Bear Jaw Trail on the left.

The Bear Jaw Trail immediately enters the mainstream of **aspen** trees. The trees' argentine trunks and glowing treetops animate the trail's atmosphere as it drops harshly into Bear Jaw Canyon. After 1 mile, the trail levels out briefly, then resumes its downhill trod on a saner grade. As the trail drops in elevation toward the route's start, more conifers enter the forest. Eventually, the trail charms its way into a level path in a pine meadow accommodating intermittent islands of **aspen** trees, then closes the loop back at the Abineau Trail. Return on the old road back to the parking area.

CREEPING BARBERRY
Berberis repens

In another century, you might have picked a spray of barberry to ward off witches. Today, you're much better off leaving their creeping stems intact and enjoying the red and maroon colors that their hollylike leaves turn to in the fall.

Look for creeping barberry to appear most often in pine forests. But you'll also find them just as comfortable in sub-alpine biomes.

The purple berries on the foot-long plants make a drink akin to lemonade. The Navajo use an infusion of its twigs and leaves to treat rheumatism.

ABINEAU–BEAR JAW LOOP

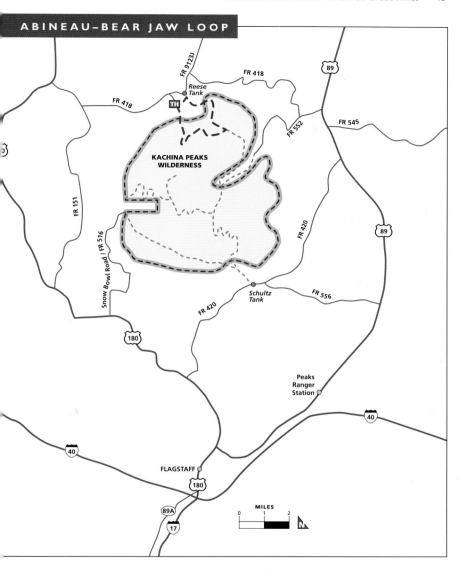

FR 9123J

FR 418

89

Reese
Tank

FR 418

TH

FR 552

FR 545

**KACHINA PEAKS
WILDERNESS**

FR 151

89

Snow Bowl Road / FR 516

FR 420

Schultz
Tank

FR 556

FR 420

180

Peaks
Ranger
Station

40

40

FLAGSTAFF

180

89A

17

MILES

0   1   2

Autumn
Hike 9 *Inner Basin Trail*

TRAIL RATING	moderate
TRAIL LENGTH	3 miles one way
LOCATION	Flagstaff
ELEVATION	8,600–10,150 feet
CONTACT	Coconino National Forest, 520-526-0866
PEAK COLOR	early October
SPECIAL ONSIDERATIONS	To protect the watershed from potential contamination, camping, horses, and dogs are not allowed in the Inner Basin.
DIRECTIONS	From Flagstaff, drive north on US 89 about 17 miles. Take a left onto FR 552 (about 1 mile north of the Sunset Crater turnoff), drive west 1.5 miles, and turn right at a sign for Lockett Meadow. Drive 3 more miles to the trailhead.

The Inner Basin Trail takes hikers into an alpine meadow that was once the heart of a 15,000-foot volcano. The San Francisco Peaks' highest mountaintops—Doyle, Fremont, Agassiz, and Humphreys—make up the caldera of the volcano that rings the meadow. In warm weather, snowmelt from the peaks and monsoon rains fill the basin and its several springs, creating a repository of water for the City of Flagstaff.

Starting on a primitive road that passes through a stand of **aspen** glowing with a rich golden display, the trail makes a nonstop ascent to Lockett Meadow. Jack Smith Spring, which pours more than a half-million gallons of water per day in the early summer months, signals that you're almost to the meadow. At the old spring house located on the edge of the basin, the San Francisco Peaks' mountain panoramas open up to you.

Once in the meadow, you can see where rock avalanches tumbled down the surrounding mountain slopes, which gleam gold from **aspen** trees. You can continue on the trail as it climbs up the side of the caldera through a corridor of spruce toward the Weatherford Trail. If you look behind you during the climb up, you'll see the rosy tinge of the Painted Desert along the eastern horizon. Return the way you came.

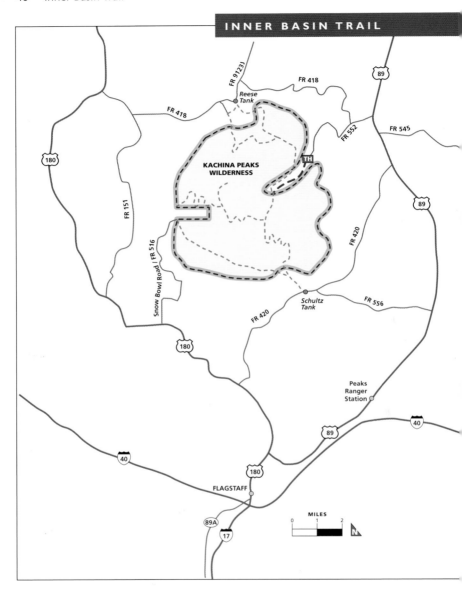

INNER BASIN TRAIL

FR 9123)

FR 418

89

Reese
Tank

FR 418

FR 552

FR 545

180

KACHINA PEAKS
WILDERNESS

TH

89

FR 151

FR 420

Snow Bowl Road / FR 516

Schultz
Tank

FR 556

FR 420

180

Peaks
Ranger
Station

40

89

40

180

FLAGSTAFF

89A

17

MILES

0   1   2

N

Kachina Trail

TRAIL RATING	moderate
TRAIL LENGTH	5 miles one way
LOCATION	Flagstaff
ELEVATION	9,800–8,900 feet
CONTACT	Coconino National Forest, 520-526-0866
PEAK COLOR	early October
DIRECTIONS	From Flagstaff, drive north on US 180 about 10 miles to the turnoff for the Snowbowl (FR 516, at mile marker 223). Turn north (right) and drive 6.2 miles to the trailhead.
SPECIAL CONSIDERATIONS	Most of the Kachina Trail is located in the Kachina Peaks Wilderness, where no mechanized vehicles, including mountain bikes, are allowed.

The San Francisco Peaks' colorful slopes rise above the meadows along Kachina Trail.

Many American Indians consider the San Francisco Peaks sacred. The Hopi Indians believe supernatural beings called Kachinas make their home in the peaks. The Kachina Trail, which contours the south face of the San Francisco Peaks, takes its name from the Kachina Peaks Wilderness, through which it passes.

The trail features a consistent glow of gold from the stands of **aspen** that congregate along its path and spread across surrounding peaks. An often shady trek that passes through mixed conifer forests, the trail also gets strong doses of sun in alpine meadows interspersed along the way.

In the forests, **aspen** leaves fall like glitter and lodge on dark green boughs of firs and atop giant charcoal-gray boulders and rockwalls stationed along the trail. Colonies of post-flowering **wild geranium** may show yellow and red colors.

Along with the carpet of gold leaves that settles on the trail, you may see imprints of elk or deer hooves sunken in the soft dark earth. If you're hiking early in the morning, you may see one of these creatures, too.

The **aspen** trees prefer to congregate around the alpine meadows, where you'll find the densest stands. During early morning or late afternoon, the soft light filtering through the trees' golden leaves produces an ethereal effect. In the larger meadows, you'll get glimpses of the surrounding countryside— Flagstaff to the south and the San Francisco Peaks to the north. In the last mile, the trail links together a chain of meadows offering frequent looks at the San Francisco Peaks' color-streaked slopes.

The trail ends in a large **aspen** grove at the intersection with the old Weatherford Road. Return the way you came.

WILD GERANIUM
Geranium caespitosum

Trees aren't the only florae to produce colorful leaves in Arizona's autumn landscapes. Since carotene and xanthophyll pigments occur in all green plants, many bushes and wildflowers turn pretty shades of yellow, gold, and red. The five-lobed leaves of the wild geranium, said to resemble a lion's paw, give the plant its alternate name of patita de leon.

Wild geraniums like the rich soil of pine forests. In the fall, their leaves can show red, yellow, and salmon hues.

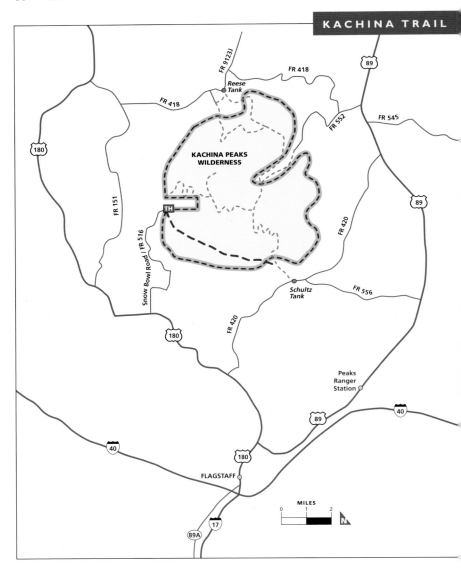

KACHINA TRAIL

Weatherford Trail

TRAIL RATING	difficult
TRAIL LENGTH	5–8.7 miles one way
LOCATION	Flagstaff
ELEVATION	8,800–12,000 feet
CONTACT	Coconino National Forest, 520-526-0866
PEAK COLOR	early October
SPECIAL CONSIDERATIONS	Most of the Weatherford Trail is located in the Kachina Peaks Wilderness, where no mechanized vehicles, including mountain bikes, are allowed. Horses are not allowed beyond the Doyle Saddle, which enters the Inner Basin watershed.
DIRECTIONS	From Flagstaff, drive north on US 180 about 5 miles to Schultz Pass Road (FR 420) and turn east (right). At the intersection with FR 557, turn north (left) and continue on FR 420 for 6 miles to the trailhead at Schultz Tank.

Once an old road built by John Weatherford in the 1920s, the trail provides a scenic and secluded route up the north side of the San Francisco Peaks, eventually climbing past Fremont, Doyle, and Agassiz Peaks to Agassiz Saddle, just shy of Humphreys Peak. Weatherford charged motoring tourists a toll to use his namesake road, which slogged up to the top of the San Francisco Peaks until the Great Depression put the kibosh on his money-making scheme.

In just over 1 mile, the trail enters a mixed conifer forest woven with **aspen** trees. The forest squeezes the trail down to a single track as it marches up a steady grade. As the trail rounds the east side of the San Francisco Peaks, you'll enjoy outstanding views of the countryside, showing brilliant stands of **aspen** trees on Schultz Peak to the north and the flush of Sedona's red rocks to the south. The path continues to ease its way up in elevation on long switchbacks with moderate grades—vacillating between glowing stands of **aspen** trees, shadowy mixed conifer forests, and sun-drenched meadows—until it finally rises above most of the **aspen** trees and into exclusively mixed conifers.

At Doyle Saddle, about mile 5, the trail approaches an extraordinary mountain scene. Here, the sparse vegetation produces a stark, but beautiful, landscape that exposes reddish rock formations and patches of gold that shine from **aspen** stands heading down into the Inner Basin. Watch for **bracted strawberry** along the trail, their three serrated-edge leaves turning shades from rose to maroon. Doyle Saddle makes a good turnaround point for a day hike.

For a longer hike, continue heading east on the trail as it contours the north face of Fremont Peak. As you pick through a boulder field down the peak's slope, eye the color of the **aspen** trees spread across neighboring mountainsides. Keeping generally level, the trail passes through a forest of Engelmann spruce and bristlecone pines, past the intersection with the Inner Basin Trail (mile 6.5), and starts a slow climb to rise above the treeline. As the air and the trees thin out, you'll see a beautiful splash of color from **aspen** trees in Abineau Canyon to the north and the rouge of the Painted Desert beyond.

When the trail starts to climb across the barren, rocky slope of Agassiz Peak, you'll see a sign informing you that off-trail hiking is prohibited to protect the endangered, and federally protected, San Francisco Peaks groundsel, found exclusively on the peaks. Finally, the trail reaches its end as it crests Agassiz Saddle, showing a pretty patchwork of **aspen** gold in the multihued green

The Weatherford Trail affords outstanding views of the aspen-dotted countryside up to the San Francisco Peaks.

landscape. You can return the way you came, or continue another 0.75 mile—and 633 feet—up the Mt. Humphreys Trail to its end, which brings you to the top of Arizona.

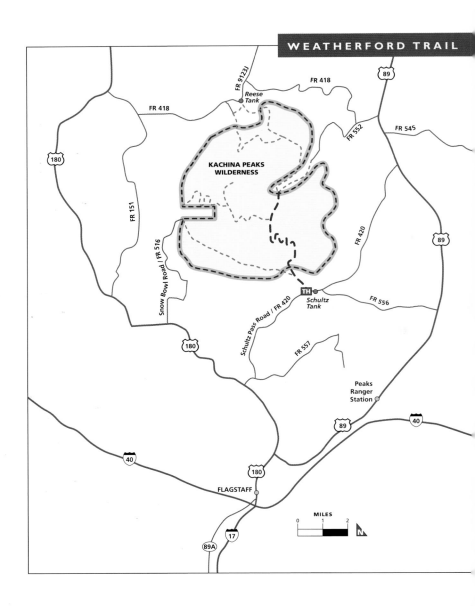

Pumphouse Wash

TRAIL RATING	difficult
TRAIL LENGTH	3.5 miles one way
LOCATION	Sedona
ELEVATION	6,400–5,690 feet
CONTACT	Coconino National Forest, 520-282-4119
PEAK COLOR	mid- to late October
SPECIAL CONSIDERATIONS	This hike has no trail and presents a challenging route. A walking stick will help you balance while hopping the rocks and boulders. Do not hike this canyon in wet weather.
DIRECTIONS	From Sedona, drive 12.6 miles north on Arizona 89A (to just over 0.5 mile past mile marker 187). Park on the road just south of the Pumphouse Wash bridge. You can arrange a shuttle by continuing north past the bridge up to the rim and 1.5 miles past the Oak Creek Overlook to FR 237. Turn east (right) and drive 1.5 miles to a parking area.

As soon as you drop into Pumphouse Wash and see its canyon floor heaped with rocks and boulders (your route), you'll know if you want to continue. The route through the canyon consists of rock and boulder hopping in the first mile, climbing around pools during the second mile, and more rock hopping with intermittent stretches of beaten path along the third mile. Much like a river hike, but without the water, the route is slow going and takes about an hour per mile.

For most experienced hikers, the route is a fun adventure. But this route can challenge a hiker's comfort level—and for some it even becomes unsafe. Hike only if you feel secure. When you start to feel uncomfortable, turn around.

For all the difficulty this canyon hike poses, it rewards you with beautiful scenery, a remote atmosphere, and an exquisite collage of fall color. The intense glow of gold from **velvet ash**, **willow**, and **boxelder** trees and sprawling **canyon grape** presents a bold beginning of color that only gets better at each turn of the bend in the serpentine wash. In the distance, you'll see bursts of red from **bigtooth maple** trees. **Virginia creeper** weaves scarlet trails across boulders the color of storm clouds.

The canyon's buff-colored Coconino sandstone walls, etched with cross-bedding as deep as a furrowed brow, rise several hundred feet above the canyon floor. Sandstone outcroppings jut into the wash like jagged gateposts chewed by erosion. Sometimes giant logjams bridge these narrow passages. Occasional

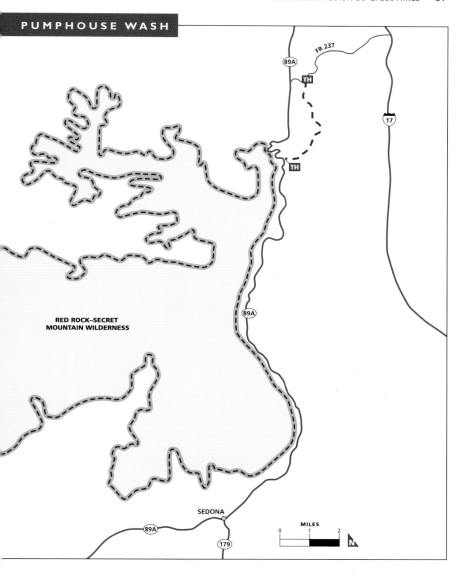

cairns stacked atop boulders suggest easier routes through the jumble of rock. In a few instances, brief sections of loose gravel or fine sand grant a reprieve from the tedious boulder hopping.

About 0.5 mile into the canyon, when a columned basalt cap appears on the canyon rim, you might hear nearby voices. The voices are tumbling down from a scenic viewpoint up on the rim.

In another 0.5 mile, you'll come to a ledge of sandstone that requires a bit of help to negotiate. You may have the advantage of previous hikers' ingenuity in the form of a stack of rocks or heavy logs to aid your climb up it. As soon as you boost yourself up, you have to edge deep cylinder-shaped holes carved by whirlpools of floodwater.

The rest of the shelf, which lasts about 1 mile, shows ornate patterns of erosion where floodwater churned, chiseled, whirled, and smoothed the rock with slots, troughs, pools, and potholes. The fall color congregates thickly in this section, and it's worth the mild-mannered canyoneering it takes to pass through it. **Red-osier dogwood** gathers in rosy and yellow-tinged pockets. **Alderleaf mountain mahogany** creates yellow cascades from cracks in the canyon walls. Still pools of water reflect yellow and red hues from **bigtooth maple** trees.

At about mile 2, the canyon curls to the northwest and makes a quick yawn that allows a douse of sunshine. A stand of ponderosa pines gathers on a small bench in the opening. The canyon immediately tapers again, and you're back to rock hopping and edging past pools. The canyon remains wide enough to accommodate benches that harbor **New Mexico locust** trees and **Fendler rose** bushes. Enjoy the added yellow color, but be careful of the thorns.

At mile 2.5, you'll come to a column arch at the bottom of the canyon where floodwaters have dissolved a portion of the canyon wall. Just beyond the arch, watch for a handful of **aspen** on the left. At this point, the canyon widens dramatically and the north wall disappears behind a forest of ponderosa pines. Look for a trail that hops onto the bench that accommodates the forest of pines. The trail travels about 0.5 mile in the forest, crosses the wash, then climbs 0.25 mile up to the rim. Return the way you came or connect with your shuttle here.

FENDLER ROSE

Rosa fendleri
There are two species of wild roses in Arizona—Fendler rose and Arizona rose. The easiest way to identify the two is by their thorns: the Fendler's are straight and the Arizona's are curved. The Fendler rose has a bigger blossom, and the bush grows three times larger than the Arizona rose, which grows to only about 3 feet. Both species respond to fall's cooler weather by turning their serrated leaves yellow, which looks especially attractive on the Fendler's reddish stems.

The tangy tasting fruit of the rose bushes, rose hips, lingers on their branches often through the winter. You can pluck the fruit right off the branch and eat it. The hips contain a relatively high amount of vitamins C and A.

Hospital Canyon

TRAIL RATING	easy
TRAIL LENGTH	0.5 mile one way
LOCATION	Sedona
ELEVATION	5,000–5,100 feet
CONTACT	Slide Rock State Park, 520-282-3034
PEAK COLOR	mid-October
SPECIAL CONSIDERATIONS	Arizona State Parks charges a $5 admission fee per car containing up to four persons.
DIRECTIONS	From Sedona, drive 6.6 miles north on Arizona 89A to Slide Rock State Park on the west side of the highway.

Once a makeshift recovery area for livestock on the Pendley Homestead, Hospital Canyon becomes a chasm full of color in the fall. The short distance and moderate incline from beginning to end make this trail a relatively easy hike for most everyone to enjoy a nice display of fall colors.

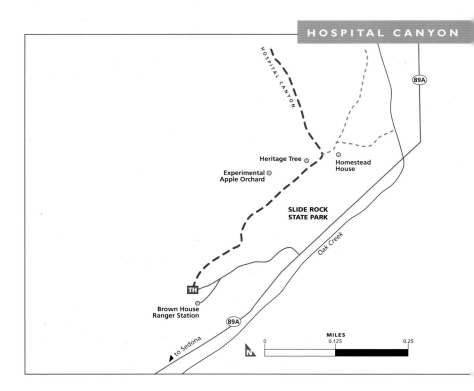

The first 0.25 mile starts on the paved Pendley Homestead Trail. Once you reach the Pendley Homestead, veer left onto a gravel pathway and veer left again at a fork. Continue on the pathway as it crosses a meadow dotted with historic apple trees. Frank Pendley planted the orchard in 1912, and the trees still supply enough fruit for bears and humans to enjoy—it's self-service for the bears, but for humans, the whole fruit and containers of fresh juice are sold at the park's Slide Rock Market.

When the pathway comes to a group of three cream-colored structures, veer right and go about 30 yards to the footpath in the canyon.

The canyon features an intimate atmosphere with warm red rockwalls cozying up to the trail as the path makes its gradual climb to the head of the boxed canyon. Along the way, a tangle of **Gambel oak**, **bigtooth maple**, and **Arizona walnut** trees crowd in the canyon and color a forest of mixed pines with hues of yellow and red. **Canyon grape** strings from pines and crawls over boulders.

The trail ends at a pour-off stuffed with **canyon grape** and **poison ivy**. **Bigtooth maple**, **Arizona walnut**, and a mixture of pines congregate around the edge of the pour-off and peer inside. Return the way you came.

Colorful oak, maple, and walnut trees highlight the mixed pine forest in Hospital Canyon.

West Fork Trail

TRAIL RATING	easy
TRAIL LENGTH	3 miles one way
LOCATION	Sedona
ELEVATION	5,400–5,500 feet
CONTACT	Coconino National Forest, 520-282-4119
PEAK COLOR	mid-October
SPECIAL CONSIDERATIONS	The Forest Service charges a $5 parking fee. This trail is located in the Red Rock–Secret Mountain Wilderness, where no mechanized vehicles, including mountain bikes, are allowed.
DIRECTIONS	From Sedona, drive 9.9 miles north on Arizona 89A to the Call of the Canyon parking area on the west side of the highway.

This trail starts in a meadow that reflects the moodiness of the fall season in Oak Creek Canyon. Signs of summer—asters, trailing four o'clocks, and prairie sunflowers—hang around the tired meadow like guests that stay too long. Their colors, muted with age, stain now-strawed grass. Fall takes precedence over the scene, embellishing it with **boxelder** and **velvet ash** trees interloping in a historic apple orchard featuring gold tones. **Canyon grape** paints golden streaks up rockwalls and trees.

The apple trees drip with ripe fruit. If you start your hike early enough in the morning, you might catch a black bear grabbing a piece for breakfast.

After the trail cuts through the meadow, it crosses a footbridge where **Virginia creeper** hangs like scarlet streamers from Arizona cypress and ponderosa pine trees. On the ground, **poison ivy** blushes red hues on golden leaves. Some plants still have their small berries, the color of old lace. Every part of the **poison ivy** plant has the potential for causing a weeping rash, any time of the year, so be careful around this prevalent bush.

Just past the bridge, you'll come to the ruins of the Mayhew Lodge, which saw the likes of Warren Harding, Clark Gable, and Carole Lombard as guests. On the right, you'll see a cellar and storage building; on the left, a stand of tree-of-heaven trees, nonnative to the canyon, surrounds the lodge ruins.

Boxelder trees form a golden corridor to the trail registry. From there, the trail leads you to the banks of the west fork of Oak Creek, which flows between the canyon's beautiful salmon sandstone walls streaked with charcoal smudges. Stepping-stones lead you across the creek where **red-osier dogwood** and **willow** thickets like to congregate. The leaves of the red-stemmed **red-osier dogwood** range from gold to maroon whereas the lance-leafed **willow** turns gold.

Before the next of many creek crossings, you'll spot the red flame of **bigtooth maple** trees. The **maples** grow thick in the canyon, boasting a host

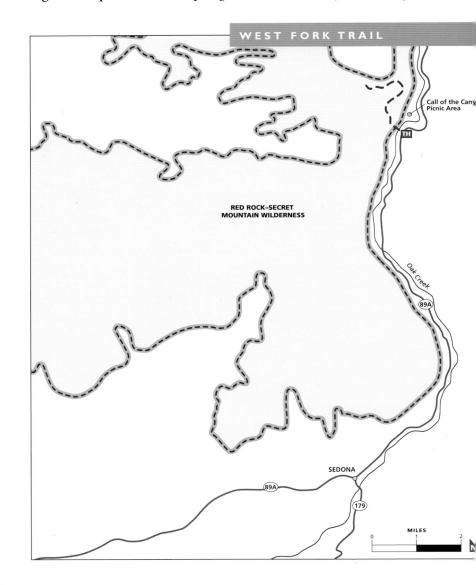

WEST FORK TRAIL

Call of the Cany
Picnic Area

TH

RED ROCK–SECRET
MOUNTAIN WILDERNESS

Oak Creek

89A

SEDONA

89A

179

MILES
0   1   2

of hues. Trees in shadier sections turn yellow while those exposed to more sun produce orange to reddish colors.

Concrete mile markers, left over from the lodge days, mark your progress along the trail. By mile 1, the trail becomes a kaleidoscope of color from turning leaves, red- and buff-colored sandstone canyon walls, and the orange glow of the trunks of older ponderosa pines. The trail parallels the creek and sometimes lingers in the creek bed, edging the waters along terra-cotta slickrock.

Halfway through the hike, the erosion-carved cliffs close in on the trail and create a more intimate feel. The creek meanders noticeably, jogging south, then west again. At the end of the jog, the trail passes an old rockfall and continues in a crowd of **bigtooth maple** trees.

At mile 2, **western hophornbeam** trees line the creek's edge. The trees' long limbs stretch over the creek water and toss a yellow glow across the surface from their soft leaves. In another 0.25 mile, you'll come to a sandstone shelf, nicknamed The Wave, that curls over the trail.

The last of the trail climbs up a bench and stays above the creek for about 0.25 mile. When the trail drops back into the creek bed, it comes to a quick end at a pool. If you don't mind getting your feet wet, you may wade through the water and continue. An unmaintained trail takes you deeper into the canyon, crossing knee- to thigh-deep water. At mile 5, a chest-deep pool makes a good turnaround point. Return the way you came.

WILLOW
Salicaceae

Of the more than 100 species of willows in the United States, more than a third of them grow in the West. From the bushy coyote willow to the giant-sized Goodding willow, all willows love water and make their homes near ready sources of groundwater. Because of similar features and constant crossbreeding, distinguishing willows can be tricky.

Many willows grow in thickets, forming an interwoven root system that helps prevent erosion. The dense growth provides browse for livestock and wild animals, but can make hiking difficult.

Basket makers around the world prefer willow branches. American Indians use the flexible twigs for basket making. In herbal medicine, willows have been used to relieve inflammation for more than 2,000 years. Modern medicine derived acetylsalicylic acid, also known as aspirin, from salicylates naturally occurring in willows. In folklore around the world, the willow is considered a sacred tree.

Autumn
Hike 15

Sterling Pass Trail

TRAIL RATING	strenuous
TRAIL LENGTH	2.4 miles one way
LOCATION	Sedona
ELEVATION	4,850–5,950 feet
CONTACT	Coconino National Forest, 520-282-4119
PEAK COLOR	late October to early November
SPECIAL CONSIDERATIONS	The Forest Service charges a $5 fee for parking in the Coconino National Forest. This trail is located in the Red Rock–Secret Mountain Wilderness, where no mechanized vehicles, including mountain bikes, are allowed.
DIRECTIONS	From Sedona, go north on Arizona 89A and drive 6.2 miles to the trailhead (on the west side of the road, 200 yards north of the Manzanita Campground).

A man named Sterling, who counterfeited money in his namesake canyon, adds a colorful slant to Sedona history. Sterling was also a cattle thief, and homesteaders in the area followed his tracks, imprinted in the snow, over a pass in the canyon in search of their chattel. The pass and canyon now memorialize Sterling's notorious name.

The tawdry Sterling picked one of the nicest canyons in the Oak Creek drainage to hang out in. In the fall, the canyon becomes filled with a passionate display of fiery colors from **bigtooth maple** trees.

The color starts out mildly as the trail dashes up a short, but steep, forested wall of Oak Creek Canyon where a handful of **Arizona walnut** and **hackberry** trees hang out. The trail settles down to a more sensible climb as it passes through an evergreen forest of pines and manzanitas brightened by **velvet ash** trees and **alderleaf mountain mahogany** bushes turned gold for the fall.

As the trail breaks from the forested cover and contours the edge of a slickrock pour-off, the **velvet ash** trees follow. The trail, with the drainage as its constant companion, then heads into a captivating forest filled with giant ponderosa pines glowing with orange trunks. This shady and moist environment attracts hardwoods that produce an outstanding show of fall color.

Gambel oak trees start the display, with **skunkbush** and tendrils of **canyon grape** punctuating it. Then **bigtooth maple** trees join in with hues of red that

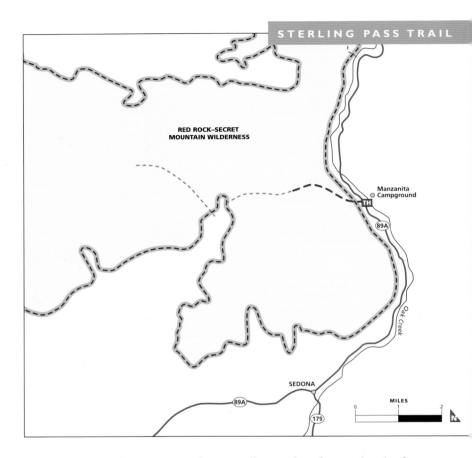

RED ROCK–SECRET
MOUNTAIN WILDERNESS

Manzanita
Campground
TH

89A

Oak Creek

SEDONA

89A

179

MILES
0   1   2

rival the surrounding Supai sandstone walls. **Bracken ferns** color the forest floor rusty orange.

The path takes on an austere temperament as it starts a steep and rugged climb out of the drainage, rising above the pines and into the sunshine. The **bigtooth maple** trees lag behind, but the **Gambel oak** trees follow. **Hackberry** trees reappear with yellowed leaves, and **sumac** bushes color the trailsides with scarlet and wine.

As the trail becomes more demanding, the panoramic views become more exquisite. A thread of color animates the gathering of hardwoods along the canyon floor while **bigtooth maples,** climbing with mixed conifers up the north-facing wall of the canyon, weave a blanket of color.

Once at the top of the pass, you can follow a beaten path that leads to a rockwall where an easy climb leads to stunning views of the Dry Creek canyon system on the west and Oak Creek Canyon to the east. Return the way you came.

TRAIL RATING	moderate
TRAIL LENGTH	5.5 miles one way
LOCATION	Sedona
ELEVATION	5,300–4,640 feet
CONTACT	Coconino National Forest, 520-282-4119
PEAK COLOR	late October to early November
SPECIAL CONSIDERATIONS	The Forest Service charges a $5 parking fee. Most of this trail is located in the Red Rock–Secret Mountain Wilderness, where no mechanized vehicles, including mountain bikes, are allowed.
DIRECTIONS	From Sedona, drive west on Arizona 89A about 3 miles to Dry Creek Road and turn right. Drive north 1.9 miles, turn northeast (right) onto FR 152, and then go about 3.2 miles to the trailhead on the left. High-clearance vehicles are best for this road.

The trail gets its start by crossing the Dry Creek streambed, which normally lives up to its name. However, in wet weather, you'll have to rock hop across it. After climbing out of the drainage, the trail immediately enters the Red Rock–Secret Mountain Wilderness. A panorama of sandstone cliffs embraces the high desert cover of manzanita, piñons, and junipers that surrounds the trail, creating a beautiful red rock backdrop for the sea of green vegetation.

Although the high desert vegetation is normally lackluster when it comes to autumn color, the vegetation along the trail is punctuated with dashes of color because it closely follows the Secret Canyon drainage, where color-producing foliage gets its necessary supply of moisture. At times, especially at and near drainage crossings, you'll see **Arizona sycamore** trees display warm tan leaves; **velvet ash**, **common hop**, **hackberry**, and **Fremont cottonwood** trees beam yellow; and **skunkbush** add hues of red and orange.

At about mile 1, the trail begins to climb gradually, pulling away from the streambed and all the color. The trail comes to a junction with the David Miller Trail at about mile 1.7. Continue on the Secret Canyon Trail, which drops in and out of the drainage, then ducks under a pine forest where the real color begins.

First you see the return of **velvet ash** trees along the trail and **Gambel oak** trees in the background. Then a burst of gold from **Arizona walnut** and

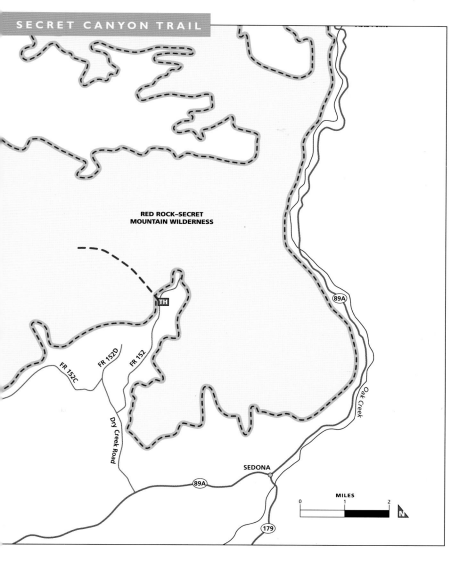

SECRET CANYON TRAIL

Fremont cottonwood trees in the drainage grabs your attention. A short foot-path on the left takes you to the edge of the canyon, where you can see the high drama of fall color stuffed in the drainage—gold coils of **canyon grape** strung around pine trees, hues of red from **bigtooth maple** trees, and warm tan leaves on **Arizona sycamore** trees.

The main trail continues up Secret Canyon, staying next to, and often in, the streambed for another mile. The path brushes up against **Arizona walnut** trees, admires **bigtooth maple** trees, and picks through colonies of **poison ivy** vibrantly colored red and gold. It passes **common hop** and **boxelder** trees that intensify the golden glow surrounding the path. **Arizona sycamore** trees beam a honey color in the sunlight. Near a distinctive rock formation on the left, watch for **western hophornbeam** trees that cascade their gold-leaved branches over the streambed next to the north face of the canyon.

At about mile 3, the trail climbs out of the drainage and onto a bench filled with a grove of **Gambel oak** trees. **Bigtooth maple** trees flaunt intense coral colors in the streambed below. When the trail descends the bench, **sumac** bushes meet it on the canyon floor, radiating orange and red tones. From this point on, the trail vacillates between bench walking and creek crossings, and **bigtooth maple** trees increase in number to ignite a continuous collage of color.

With such a strong display of fall color, don't forget to enjoy the surrounding Supai and Coconino sandstone cliffs, which rise more than 1,000 feet above the canyon floor. When you reach the trail's end at several pools, return the way you came.

CANYON GRAPE
Vitis arizonica

In the fall, streamers of canyon grape make a stunning sight with their three-lobed maplelike leaves adding golden flecks to the trees. The woody vine of canyon grape, which takes to streamsides and canyons, also sprawls over bushes and rocks.

Small animals and birds pluck the dark purple fruit, which matures in late summer. Some Indians used to eat the fruit raw and store sun-dried reserves. The tiny, tart fruit makes good preserves, juice, and wine.

Packed with minerals and tartaric acid, the alkaline fruit is said to aid the body in clearing toxins, neutralizing uric acid, and ridding stones from the kidneys. To allay thirst, natives chewed the raw leaves and also used the leaves as poultices on snakebites.

Huckaby Trail

Larry Ulrich

TRAIL RATING	easy
TRAIL LENGTH	2.5 miles one way
LOCATION	Sedona
ELEVATION	4,400–4,550 feet
CONTACT	Coconino National Forest, 520-282-4119
PEAK COLOR	mid- to end of October
SPECIAL CONSIDERATIONS	A $5 parking fee is required at this trailhead. You may arrange a shuttle at the Midgely Bridge parking area just north of downtown Sedona on Arizona 89A.
DIRECTIONS	From Sedona, take Arizona 179 south for 0.5 mile. Turn east (left) onto Schnebly Hill Road and drive 0.9 mile to the trailhead.

Built as a wagon road in 1887, the Huckaby Trail got its name from Jim Huckaby, who lived just opposite the Midgely Bridge along Oak Creek. The trail offers a different perspective on Sedona and its surrounding red rock hillsides as it peers, with an innuendo of remoteness, at the activity of the town from the eastern rim of Oak Creek Canyon.

From the Schnebly Hill Road trailhead, the trail descends quickly into Bear Wallow Wash, then climbs for 0.5 mile up to a ridge that grants outstanding views of several formations around town. The trail levels off and curves around Mitten Ridge, exposing a bold gold ribbon of **Fremont cottonwood** and **velvet ash** trees that follows Oak Creek in the canyon below. The trail then drops into the canyon and parallels Oak Creek, traveling over terra-cotta-colored slickrock and sandy paths in a riparian cover of **Arizona sycamore**, **Fremont cottonwood**, and pine trees.

At mile 2, the trail makes its first creek crossing; the second is another 0.25 mile farther. You have to rock hop or wade each crossing. As the trail switchbacks up to the Midgely Bridge parking area, you're greeted by a full view of the face of massive Steamboat Rock, which overlooks the bridge. Once in the parking area, look back at the golden glow of color along the creek. If you have not set up a shuttle, return the way you came.

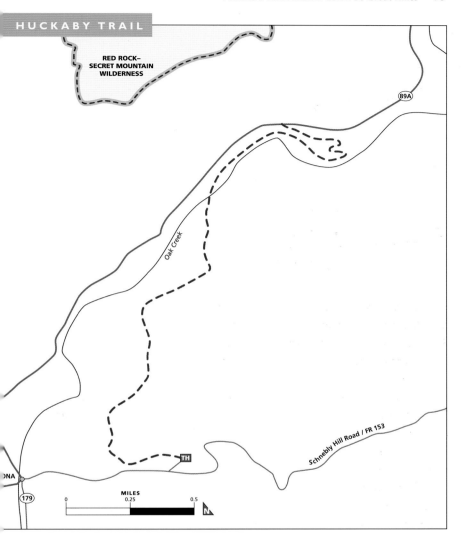

HUCKABY TRAIL

RED ROCK–
SECRET MOUNTAIN
WILDERNESS

89A

Oak Creek

Schnebly Hill Road / FR 153

TH

DNA

179

MILES
0   0.25   0.5

N

*Autumn
Hike 18* Bear Sign Trail

TRAIL RATING	moderate
TRAIL LENGTH	3.5 miles one way
LOCATION	Sedona
ELEVATION	4,800–5,400 feet
CONTACT	Coconino National Forest, 520-282-4119
PEAK COLOR	late October to early November
SPECIAL ONSIDERATIONS	The Forest Service charges a $5 parking fee at this trailhead. This trail is located in the Red Rock–Secret Mountain Wilderness, where no mechanized vehicles, including mountain bikes, are allowed.
DIRECTIONS	From Sedona, drive west on Arizona 89A about 3 miles to Dry Creek Road. Take a right and drive north 1.9 miles to FR 152, then take another right and drive northeast about 4.4 miles to the Dry Creek Trailhead on the left. High-clearance vehicles are best for this road.

This hike starts out on the Dry Creek Trail in a more remote part of the Red Rock–Secret Mountain Wilderness. The trail passes through high desert vegetation, which generally lacks any fall color. However, because the trail parallels Dry Creek, it has a tease of color from the **willow**, **velvet ash**, **Fremont cottonwood**, and **Arizona sycamore** trees that line the streambed and sometimes venture out along the trail.

In the first 0.25 mile, the trail passes through a stand of Arizona cypress, an evergreen with mottled shaggy bark. Arizona cypress trees prefer a moister environment than the piñon and juniper trees that also occupy high desert biomes. Dubbed "the keepers of the forest" by the Indians who once lived in the Sedona area, these evergreens stubbornly hang onto life, often sprouting a new limb from barren trunks. Some of the **Arizona sycamore** trees in this stretch inch their way into the cypress trees' shade.

At the first stream crossing at mile 0.5, watch for feathery **tamarisk** bushes that display a rusty gold color. In another 0.25 mile, the trail enters an exceptionally beautiful area when it drops into the streambed next to red sandstone canyon walls. **Fremont cottonwood** trees and a colony of **poison ivy** painted in bold scarlet, gold, and orange hues color the area. The trail picks through the streambed to an island of red rock that creates a fork. Veer left for the Bear Sign Trail.

The trail passes a line of **velvet ash** and **willow** trees before it climbs above the streambed into another stand of Arizona cypress. Still, you can see the burnt orange leaves of **Arizona sycamore** trees and gold from **Fremont cottonwood** trees beaming from the drainage. The trail quickly drops into the cozy canyon, now packed with golden fall color. In a short distance, you spot the rose flame of **bigtooth maple** trees.

About halfway into the hike, the color dwindles when the canyon opens up and fills with Arizona cypress. The surrounding cliffs rise powerfully several hundred feet above the canyon floor. A feeling of remoteness starts to impose on the trail. Because of this solitude, you have a good chance of finding black bear signs—or even spotting one of the bruins—along the path, giving credence to the trail's name.

The fall color resumes at about mile 2, when the trail climbs a little and the canyon walls narrow. **Arizona sycamore** and **Gambel oak** trees are the first to appear. Soon after, you see **bigtooth maple**, **Arizona walnut**, and **common hoptrees**. **Skunkbushes** add reddish hues, **canyon grape** drapes over pine trees, and **creeping barberry** colors the forest floor.

When the trail climbs up a bench on the left side of the drainage, watch for **hackberry** trees. Resembling their cousin elms, the **hackberry** trees display leaves with the sawtooth-edged elm

COMMON HOPTREE
Ptelea trifoliata

The three-part leaves of the common hoptree add a bright yellow glow to rocky slopes in the fall. A member of the rue family, along with grapefruit and orange, the hoptree resembles hops in several ways.

The small fruit, round disks reminiscent of hops, have a bitter taste and make a good substitute for hops in brewing. The leaves emit an odor like hops, too.

Herbalists use parts of the common hoptree to treat indigestion. The bark contains an alkaloid called berberine, which makes a good mild tonic.

If you come across the tree, be careful handling it. The plant can be irritating to some people.

appearance. Once the trail drops back into the drainage, **sumac** bushes appear, adding vibrant oranges and reds to the yellow fall color glowing between the red rock canyon walls.

The trail comes to a junction with the David Miller Trail at about mile 2.5. Continue on the Bear Sign Trail, which follows the drainage as it bends right. More **bigtooth maple** trees appear as the trail starts to climb into a moister environment, eventually making a stunning display. **Poison ivy** proliferates, too, so tread carefully. **Canyon grape** climbs to the treetops, the maple-like leaves fluorescing in the sunshine.

When the trail suddenly fades at about mile 3.5, return the way you came.

BEAR SIGN TRAIL

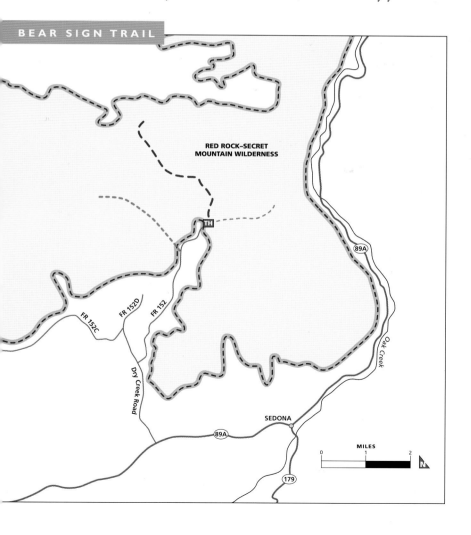

Crescent Moon Trail

Short and easy, the Crescent Moon Trail provides a relaxed hike in an idyllic atmosphere set in the red rock country just west of Sedona. The trail features a variety of interesting sights as it takes you past an old homestead built by John Lee in the late 1800s and through a lush riparian environment along Oak Creek that kindles with fall color. The route ends across from Cathedral Rock in a gathering of prayer rocks.

A paved walkway, which loops around a large meadow where the Lee homestead's cabin and mill stand, takes you past sweet-smelling **Arizona sycamore** trees wearing light tan leaves, **sumac** turned deep maroon, and **Fremont cottonwood** trees beaming gold. Then **Arizona walnut** and **velvet ash** trees join in the mix, adding golden hues.

At the far end of the paved loop, take the dirt path on the right that enters a dense riparian area where **boxelder** and **Texas mulberry** show up gold among still-green **thinleaf alder** trees. The ready supply of water encourages

TRAIL RATING	easy
TRAIL LENGTH	0.5 mile one way
LOCATION	Sedona
ELEVATION	4,500 feet
CONTACT	Recreation Resource Management, 520-203-0624
PEAK COLOR	late October
SPECIAL CONSIDERATIONS	Part of the trail is handicapped accessible. The Forest Service charges a $5 admission fee.
DIRECTIONS	From Sedona, go west on Arizona 89A and drive about 5 miles (just past mile marker 370) to Upper Red Rock Loop (FR 216) and turn left. Drive 1.8 miles to Chavez Ranch Road and turn left; drive 0.7 mile to the signed entrance.

the trees and shrubs to grow to larger-than-normal heights. **Blackberry** brambles mound along either side of the trail, their summer green fading to yellow and pale red; and **sumac**, usually growing only 5–7 feet high, reach their full potential of 20 feet here. Gigantic **Arizona sycamore** and **cottonwood** trees splay their branches, spreading from imposing trunks, across the trail.

Velvet ash trees follow the trail when it pulls away from the creek and momentarily steps out of the riparian cocoon of color, then rushes back into it. The path finally exits the riparian cover at about mile 0.3 and clatters across a several-hundred-foot-long slab of slickrock toward a stunning view of Cathedral Rock, a signature formation of Sedona. **Fremont cottonwood** and **Arizona sycamore** trees flank the creek banks, tossing golden leaves and reflections into Oak Creek.

At the end of the slickrock, follow a footpath another 0.25 mile to a rock-ribbed clearing, nicknamed Buddha Beach, which is studded with arbitrarily placed stacks of rocks called prayer rocks. The prayer rocks enshrine a vortex said to exist at Cathedral Rock. Supposedly, the waters of Oak Creek that pass the base of the vortex hold healing powers; people from around the world visit the site. Once you receive your healing—or at least take a moment to enjoy the beautiful environment along Oak Creek—return the way you came.

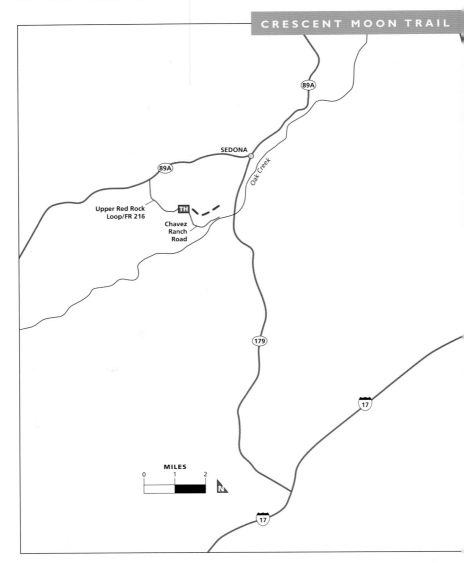

CRESCENT MOON TRAIL

Parsons Trail

TRAIL RATING	moderate
TRAIL LENGTH	4 miles one way
LOCATION	Cottonwood
ELEVATION	3,800–3,600 feet
CONTACT	Coconino National Forest, 520-282-4119
PEAK COLOR	early to mid-November
SPECIAL CONSIDERATIONS	Watch for flash floods in wet weather.
DIRECTIONS	From the junction of Arizona 260 and 89A in Cottonwood, continue on Arizona 89A north. Drive 1 mile and turn north (right) onto Historic 89A. Drive 1.9 miles through Old Town Cottonwood and turn east (right) at the Tuzigoot turnoff. Drive 0.5 mile to FR131/Sycamore Canyon Road and turn north (left), and then drive 6.7 miles on the mostly unpaved road and veer left at a fork. Drive 3 miles to the trailhead. This road is best suited for high-clearance vehicles.

The Parsons Trail starts on Sycamore Canyon's rim, overlooking the strong strand of gold interwoven with threads of green from the trees on the canyon floor along Sycamore Creek. As the trail drops down the sun-drenched wall of the canyon into the drainage, you may catch drops of color on **skunkbushes** mixed in with the evergreen high desert vegetation.

Once on the canyon floor, the trail plods on a sandy terra-cotta path that never strays far from creek banks that glow gold from **Fremont cottonwood, willow,** and **velvet ash** trees. **Arizona sycamore** trees display honey colors. You might see a few leftover wildflowers, such as yellow and red skyrockets, adding their own jewel tones to the path. And you might hear the chatter of belted kingfishers as they swoop from treetop perches over the creek.

In about 0.5 mile, the canyon's scruffy red and white walls start to impose on the trail as the gorge narrows. This creates a moister environment that attracts **Arizona walnut** and **hackberry** trees strung with **canyon grape**. At about mile 1.5, grassy banks hint of Summers Spring pooling on the left. The trees become more sumptuous—taller and fuller—and form a rich gold canopy over the trail. **Blackberry** brambles, the leaves of which may mottle yellow and pale red, grow in this particularly moist area, where **Arizona walnut** trees also flourish.

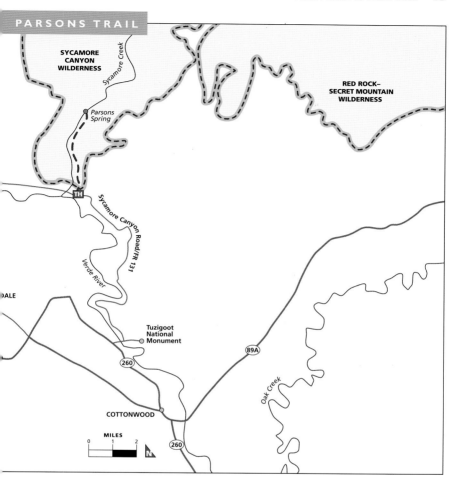

In another 0.25 mile, watch for a rock slide on your right that has crumbled from a basalt outcropping. If you're backpacking, a permanent cairn on your left indicates the first of six creek crossings you must make before you can camp. For a day hike, this is the first of five crossings to the maintained trail's end.

The trail approaches the second stream crossing in 0.25 mile. The trail takes you from the left side of the creek to the right, past a bold outcropping that juts into a pool in the creek. Then the trail climbs about 70 feet above the creek bed, now a jumble of gold and green.

The trail spends the next mile comfortably edging along ledges, picking through minor trail washouts, and touching base a couple of times with the canyon floor before it arrives at the next creek crossing. During this segment, the canyon walls display a collection of textures: red and white sandstone spires, globs of conglomerate, and columns of basalt.

In shady areas where the trail cleaves to the canyon wall, the canyon floor crawls with **canyon grape**, **Virginia creeper**, and **poison ivy** that add gold and scarlet colors along the path. Watch for **Texas mulberry** trees around mile 2.75 where the canyon walls narrow and force the trail onto a ledge. The topside of the odd-shaped **Texas mulberry** leaves feel like sandpaper.

The third creek crossing comes at about mile 3, with the fourth crossing close behind, bringing you back to the right side of the creek. The trail tramps along the sandy creek banks feeling as remote as it can get, with only the jabber of birds to keep you company.

After the fifth creek crossing at mile 3.5, the trail takes to a ledge on the left side of the creek for about 0.5 mile before it drops back into the drainage and ends at a pool of water. Parsons Spring bubbles up from the rockwall on the left. Return the way you came.

ALDERLEAF MOUNTAIN MAHOGANY
Cercocarpus montanus

The diminutive-toothed leaves of the alderleaf mountain mahogany turn a yellow color in the fall. The bush grows on high desert hillsides where evergreen vegetation prevails or it cascades from ledges on canyon walls. Fuzzy tails on its fruit that look like slender wavy feathers identify the bush in the fall and winter. The feathery tails explain another of its names, featherbush.

Though brittle and easy to crack, the hard wood of the alderleaf mountain mahogany makes it difficult to hack with an ax. The durability gives meaning to yet another one of its names, "palo duro," which means "hard wood" in Spanish. Navajos use the plant to produce a red dye for basketry, medicine, and ceremonial equipment in the Mountain Chant, Plume Way, and Chiricahua Wind Way ceremonies.

North Mingus Trail

TRAIL RATING	strenuous
TRAIL LENGTH	Up to 5.5 miles one way
LOCATION	Jerome
ELEVATION	7,800–6,200 feet
CONTACT	Prescott National Forest, 520-567-4121
PEAK COLOR	early to mid-October
SPECIAL CONSIDERATIONS	This hike makes a good shuttle. To arrange for one, park a car at a parking area along Arizona 89A located between mileposts 339 and 338 about 5 miles west of Jerome.
DIRECTIONS	From Jerome, take Arizona 89A west toward Prescott. Drive about 7.5 miles to the Mingus Mountain Recreation Center turnoff (FR 104) and turn southeast (left). Drive a total of 3 miles (through the Mingus Campground, veering left at a fork, then past the Mingus Work Center) to the trailhead.

At the start of this trail, you might catch hang gliders positioning themselves at the world-class hang gliding ramp next to the trailhead. From here, hang gliders dive into a thrilling expanse of the Verde Valley 7,800 feet below. Even without a show of hang gliders, the panorama makes an impressive sight.

The trail continues on its way, edging the rim of Mingus Mountain where **Gambel oak** trees color a meadow of ponderosa pines. **Creeping barberry** embellish the ground with hues of wine and scarlet. Within 0.5 mile, the trail drops below the rim and cuts a path through a thick stand of **Gambel oak** trees that blankets the top of the mountain.

In another 0.25 mile, the trail enters a noticeably cooler microclimate that harbors a stand of **aspen** and other colorful vegetation. **Velvet ash** leaves beam a vibrant yellow–yellow green, depending on their stage of color; **alderleaf mountain mahogany** leaves fade to a pale yellow; and **New Mexican raspberry** leaves beam their hue of gold. When the trail comes to an avalanche of gray volcanic cobbles, watch for bunches of scallop-leaved **coral bells** blushing scarlet.

The trail passes in and out of the microclimate a couple times as it switchbacks down the mountainside. **Bigtooth maple** trees appear at the last pass through the microclimate, sparingly at first, because the trail levels off and heads to the exposed eastern edge of the mountain. Here the trail intersects with Trail 105A, which the locals call the Crossover Trail. The path then doubles

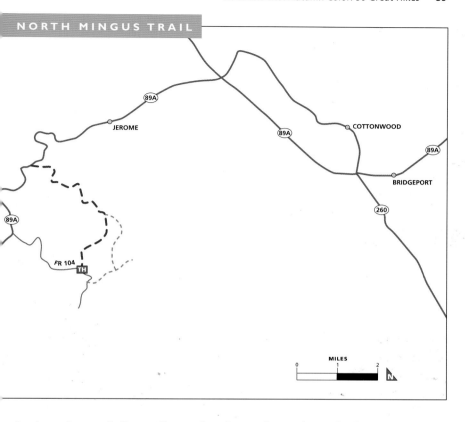

NORTH MINGUS TRAIL

back to the north face and a cooler clime of mixed conifer forest where **bigtooth maple** trees proliferate, forming, along with **Gambel oak** and **velvet ash** trees, a colorful corridor.

As the trail continues on a downward slope, it passes from the forest into a more exposed area. You can see better views of the surrounding mountain slopes featuring a rich tapestry of color. On the northern horizon, you can see the multi-strata escarpment of the Mogollon Rim crowned by the San Francisco Peaks and Bill Williams Mountain. Jerome's signature reddish-brown outcroppings poke through an evergreen high desert cover of mixed pine and juniper trees. The red rock hues of the Verde Valley glow in between.

Just past a fenced mine, the trail joins a jeep track that takes you by an old homestead ruin at Mescal Spring surrounded by **boxelder** and **velvet ash** trees. The route continues almost 1 mile to Arizona 89A. At the spring, you may return the way you came, or continue to the highway if you have arranged a shuttle.

Autumn Hike 22 ## View Point Trail

The View Point Trail has a number of visual treats that are greatly enhanced by the fall color carpeting the mountains surrounding the trail. Stretching panoramas showcase the Verde Valley, and attractive outcroppings and chasms punctuate the trail's route as it contours the east face of Mingus Mountain.

The trail starts off in the Mingus Mountain Recreation Area campground, immediately dropping below the rim into a golden stand of **Gambel oak** trees. Besides the panorama of the Verde Valley, the trail peers into a small chasm full of **bigtooth maple** trees that speckle the cleft with fiery colors.

The path descends about 1 mile down the mountain, all the while viewing the patchwork of myriad hues of gold, an exceptional showing of scarlet, and different shades of green from **velvet ash**, **Gambel oak**,

TRAIL RATING	strenuous
TRAIL LENGTH	3 miles one way
LOCATION	Jerome
ELEVATION	7,800–6,000 feet
CONTACT	Prescott National Forest, 520-567-4121
PEAK COLOR	early October
DIRECTIONS	From Jerome, take Arizona 89A toward Prescott and drive about 7.5 miles to the Mingus Mountain Recreation Center turnoff (FR 104). Turn southeast (left) and drive 2.3 miles to the trailhead in Mingus Campground.

VIEW POINT TRAIL

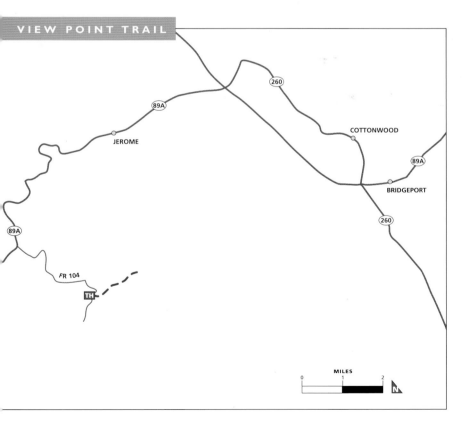

bigtooth maple, and mixed conifer trees on surrounding slopes. Scenic outcroppings punctuate the colorful scene.

The trail finally levels off and spends another mile contouring the east side of the mountain. Above the trail, bands of russet and gold run across rocky outcroppings while the Verde Valley spreads below. When the trail ducks into a forest of mixed conifers, you see colorful **skunkbush** interspersed along it. Closely related to **poison ivy**, the leaves turn to hues ranging from salmon to scarlet in the fall. **Skunkbush's** name comes from the strong scent the leaves give off when crushed. Indian women often used the stems for basket making.

At its intersection with Trail 105A, unnamed by the Forest Service but coined the Crossover Trail by the locals, the trail takes a downward plunge. Before continuing, look up at the mountaintop where you will see a fiery display of **bigtooth maples**.

Just past the intersection, the trail stoops momentarily under the cover of **Gambel oaks**. In about 0.5 mile, the path reaches a crevice full of **bigtooth maples** that drench the path in hues of red. The trail continues, without much color, about another 0.5 mile to its end at Alan Spring Road.

SKUNKBUSH
Rhus trilobata

When crushed, the lobed leaves of skunkbush emit a strong smell that some might find fragrant. Others find the scent to be more on the odious side, giving credence to its name. In the fall, these odoriferous leaves add delightful hues of yellow, salmon, and red to canyon hillsides.

Part of the cashew family, the skunkbush has some characteristics of sumac, another cashew member, inasmuch as it produces velvety red berries. Like the sumac berries, the skunkbush berries are used to make a lemonade-like drink.

Indians used the berries to make pemmican, a combination of dried meat, melted fat, and fruit. Indian women often used the stems to create baskets, giving rise to its alternate, but provocative, name of squawbush.

Verde River Greenway

TRAIL RATING	easy
TRAIL LENGTH	1.5 mile loop
LOCATION	Dead Horse Ranch State Park, Cottonwood
ELEVATION	3,300 feet
CONTACT	Dead Horse Ranch State Park, 520-634-5283
PEAK COLOR	mid- to late November
SPECIAL CONSIDERATIONS	Arizona State Parks charges a $4 admission fee for vehicles with up to four persons.
DIRECTIONS	From the junction of Arizona 260 and 89A in Cottonwood, continue on Arizona 89A north. Drive 1 mile and turn north (right) onto Historic 89A. Drive 1.3 miles through Old Town Cottonwood and turn north (right) onto 10th Street. Drive 0.8 mile to the park entrance, and then drive 0.6 mile—just past the turnoff for the ranger residence—and turn right into the West Lagoon Parking Area. The trail is located on the southeast side of the lot.

Since the turn of the last century, this land was a working farm. The Ireys family from California bought the ranch in 1951 and christened it with its curious name. The family was searching for a ranch to buy in the Verde Valley, and this one happened to have a dead horse lying on the road near the ranch. When the family discussed what land to buy, the kids chimed in they should buy the place "with the dead horse on it." The children's clamor became the ranch's name. The Ireys family sold the Dead Horse Ranch to Arizona State Parks in 1973—under the condition that the name stayed with the land.

Despite its foreboding name, the area revolves around life on the Verde River, one of the last free-flowing rivers in the Sonoran Desert. The Verde River Greenway travels 6 miles along the Verde River. This smaller loop hike offers a leisurely look at the golden fall color from the river's **Fremont cottonwood/willow** riparian forest, one of less than 20 such habitats in the world (five of which are in Arizona).

The loop hike starts as a double track trail in a meadow, traveling about 0.1 mile on the outer perimeter of the meadow along a fence line, then veers left at a junction. From here, the path bears an unusually peaceful atmosphere that makes for a pleasant hike.

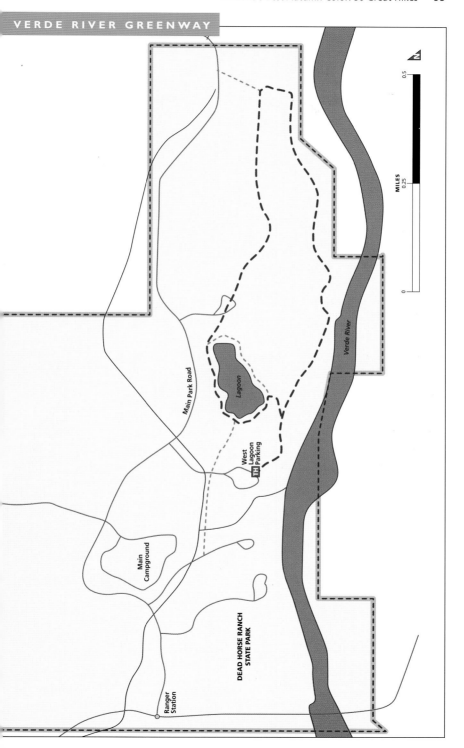

VERDE RIVER GREENWAY

DEAD HORSE RANCH STATE PARK

Verde River

Main Park Road

Lagoon

West Lagoon Parking

Main Campground

Ranger Station

MILES

0.25

0.5

Close enough to the Verde River for you to hear the splash of active birds, the trail travels under a loosely-knit canopy of **Fremont cottonwood** trees. Up above, a hawk might be circling the meadows on the other side of the trail. In the distance, you can see the surrounding red and white sandstone cliffs.

The trail's fall color comes mainly from **Fremont cottonwood** and **Goodding willow** trees. However, **boxelder** trees and **tamarisk** bushes also add hues of gold.

When the trail reaches a gravel parking area, continue on the loop that crosses the parking area and follows along a beaten path located on the lagoon dyke. **Goodding willow** trees paint the lagoon's shores gold while tossing a glow on its waters. On an early morning hike, you might spy an eagle diving for breakfast in the lagoon.

Even if you don't spot an eagle, you'll probably see fishermen casting for trout. The park's lagoon and portions of the Verde River get stocked with trout, making the park one of the best-kept secrets for trout fishing in the area.

At the end of the lagoon, cross a wooden footbridge and follow the path back to the parking area and your vehicle.

Goodding willow trees make golden the edge of a lagoon along the Verde River Greenway.

Bell Trail

George Wuerthner

TRAIL RATING	moderate
TRAIL LENGTH	3.25 miles one way
LOCATION	Wet Beaver Wilderness, Sedona
ELEVATION	3,820—4,320 feet
CONTACT	Coconino National Forest, 520-282-4119
PEAK COLOR	late October
SPECIAL CONSIDERATIONS	Except for the first mile, this trail lies in the Wet Beaver Wilderness, where no mechanized vehicles, including mountain bikes, are allowed.
DIRECTIONS	From the intersection of I-17 and Arizona 179, go southeast on FR 618 and drive 2 miles. Turn left (following signs to the trail) and continue 0.25 mile to the trail.

In 1932, Charlie Bell pioneered the Bell Trail as a route to move his cattle from the lowlands of the Verde Valley to the top of the Mogollon Rim. The trail travels almost 11 miles, but you'll find the best show of fall color on the most popular segment, which takes you to Bell's Crossing along Wet Beaver Creek.

The trail starts in the wide mouth of the canyon on an old road. Red rock cliffs capped with a layer of basalt rise on the left, and a thicket of juniper and mesquite trees separates the trail from Wet Beaver Creek on the right. **Fremont cottonwood** and **Arizona sycamore** trees hang out along the creek behind the evergreen thicket. Once the trail reaches a clearing where a large meadow divides the trail from the drainage, you're treated to a nice view of the fall color lining the creek.

Velvet ash trees hang at the edges of the meadow and near the trail, and **canyon grape** vines entwine in their branches.

By mile 0.5, the south canyon wall starts to push the creek closer to the trail, and the fall color breaks through the evergreen wall. Towering **Fremont cottonwood** trees reach above the path and sprinkle golden leaves on the terra- cotta terrain. **Arizona sycamore** trees dangle honey-colored leaves from silver white trunks lining the creek, and **velvet ash** trees weave glints of gold throughout the cover.

You may notice foot-paths branching off the trail and leading into the canopy of color. All these paths lead you to the creek a short distance away. The creek's emerald waters pour over red rock cascades and past slickrock terraces.

At mile 1.5, the trail passes the White Mesa Trail on your left. The high desert vegetation prevails as the creek sinks below the trail. The color, however, never gets too far away as to disappear completely.

At mile 2, the trail passes the Apache Maid Trail on your left. In another 0.25 mile, you'll come to a fork in the trail where the Weir Trail comes in. Veer to the left to continue on the Bell Trail.

From this point, the trail starts to climb up the north wall of the canyon, a scenic route that brushes right against bold red rock outcroppings in the wall. The trail makes itself at home along a ledge in the wall several hundred feet above the creek, where it shows off an uninhibited view of the band of gold following the creek.

Just past mile 3, the path dips into Bell's Crossing where it crosses Wet Beaver Creek and continues its steep climb up the Mogollon Rim. This exceptionally pretty area has deep pools sunk between stunning red rock walls. **Willow** thickets add more gold to the creek's riparian cover.

From Bell's Crossing, you may continue on the Bell Trail or return the way you came.

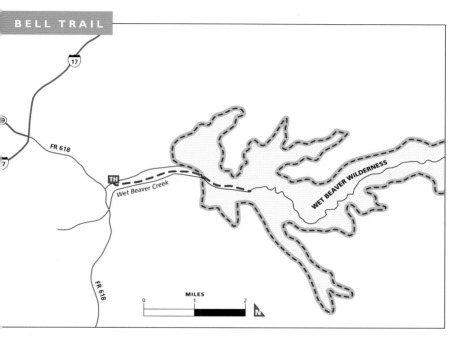

Autumn
Hike 25 *Fossil Creek Trail*

TRAIL RATING	strenuous
TRAIL LENGTH	3.5 miles one way
LOCATION	Fossil Springs Wilderness, Payson
ELEVATION	5,800—4,300 feet
CONTACT	Tonto National Forest, 520-474-7900
PEAK COLOR	late October
SPECIAL CONSIDERATIONS	The last 0.5 mile of this trail is located in the Fossil Springs Wilderness, where no mechanized vehicles, including mountain bikes, are allowed.
DIRECTIONS	From Payson, drive north on Arizona 87 about 18 miles to the town of Strawberry. Turn west (left) onto Fossil Creek Road (FR 708) and drive 4.5 miles to the signed trailhead turnoff.

The trail starts on an old road, once used to deliver materials to build the dam and flume that route water to the Irving Power Plant at trail's end. Passing through a high desert vegetation of mostly juniper and scrub oak, the trail drops 1,500 feet in 3 miles into the Fossil Creek drainage. Even in this evergreen landscape, fall color forges its way as **skunkbush** and **alderleaf mountain mahogany** bushes add yellow and red hues, and crevices harbor the gold of **Gambel oak, velvet ash,** and **common hoptrees.**

In the first 0.5 mile at the turn of a bend, a stand of **Gambel oak** mixed with **velvet ash** trees fills a crevice with gold. A little farther, the trail faces an unabashed panorama of the canyon and the colorful spired strata of the Mogollon Rim. Bold speckles of gold from **Gambel oak, common hop,** and **velvet ash** trees liven up the nubby carpet of juniper and piñon trees covering the canyon walls.

Near the canyon bottom at about mile 2.75, you pass through an S-gate. About 500 feet farther, you approach a trail junction. Turn left to head toward the Irving Power Plant.

If there's been wet weather recently, you'll have to rock hop when you reach the drainage. You might catch deer splashing in shallow pools. The dependable water source from the springs attracts a variety of wildlife from ring-tailed cats to mountain lions, javelina, and black bear.

The trail crosses Fossil Creek's bed and keeps to the north side of the drainage while barging through a plethora of color. Colonies of shoulder-high **sumac** flame red, **Fremont cottonwood** and **velvet ash** trees add tones of gold, and the leaves of **Arizona sycamore** trees glisten like honey.

At about mile 3.5, you see the first of several springs gushing into a pool of teal-tinged water canopied by an overstory of **velvet ash**, **boxelder**, **Arizona sycamore**, and **thinleaf alder**. **Alder** leaves do not turn color, but merely brown out and drop. From here, you can pick your way across rocks in the water to a footpath along the south side of the creek or continue on the main trail, which stays to the right.

The main trail enters a streamside overstory thick enough to dim the sunlight to a twilight glow. Thirty species of trees grow here, making this wilderness one of the most diverse riparian ecosystems in Arizona. On the right, desert scrub climbs up the canyon's sun-drenched hillsides to layers of limestone and sandstone. On the left, a blanketlike thicket of **blackberries** forms a magnificent mound that dips and heaves along the forest floor.

Watch for a couple of fig trees near the trail in the **blackberry** thicket. Neither the fig trees nor **blackberries** are native to the canyon but are remnants of a homestead that once stood in the vicinity. Beaten paths dangle off of the main trail and drop through the berry thicket into the drainage. Take one of the paths for a look at the springs as they bubble about 20,000 gallons of water per minute out of the limestone shelf.

BOXELDER
Acer negundo

With compound leaves that produce a golden color in the fall, boxelder trees make an important contribution to the seasonal show of colors. The boxelder, a member of the maple family, produces a sweet sap once tapped by Indians and pioneers to make syrup and sugar. The sap, however, does not have the quality produced by sugar maple trees.

These quick-growing trees have a soft wood that breaks and rots easily, lending to a short life span. Look for boxelders in moist areas, especially canyons.

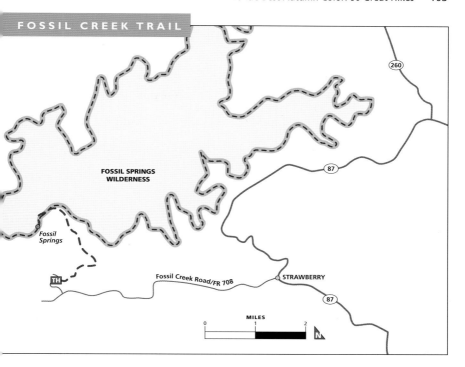

FOSSIL CREEK TRAIL

    The trail rises above the stream and its riparian cover into full sun, ending at the Irving Power Plant dam where the highly mineralized water forms a travertine accretion as it slides down the spillway. The Irving Power Plant, built in 1916, once supplied electricity to Phoenix when the city's population swelled to 30,000 people. Still in use by Arizona Public Service, the plant is scheduled to be decommissioned in 2004. The power plant is listed in the National Register of Historic Places.

    You may return the way you came or, for a different perspective, drop into the drainage on a beaten path just behind the power plant and wade the tepid creek (the waters remain 72 degrees F. all year round) to a beaten path on the other side. The path travels right next to the creek and brushes past a more vibrant display of fall color than the other side of the canyon offers. **Bigtooth maple** trees, **Virginia creeper** vines, and **sumac** bushes add warm red hues to the gold and green cover of **Fremont cottonwood** and **thinleaf alder** trees.

    When the beaten path ends, cross the creek and hike 3 miles back to the trailhead.

Autumn
Hike 26

Pine Canyon Trail

Larry Ulrich

TRAIL RATING strenuous

TRAIL LENGTH 3.5–8 miles one way

LOCATION Mogollon Rim

ELEVATION 7,200–5,000 feet

CONTACT Tonto National Forest, 520-474-7900

PEAK COLOR mid-October

DIRECTIONS From Pine, drive north on Arizona 87 about 1.1 miles past its junction with Arizona 260. Turn south (right) and proceed through the gate 0.1 mile to a parking area at the trailhead. (Be sure to close the gate.) To arrange a shuttle hike, leave a vehicle at the signed trailhead just south of the town of Pine.

The trail starts on an old road that takes you through a ponderosa pine forest to the edge of the Mogollon Rim. From there, it doesn't take long for the trail to drop into its namesake canyon, zigzagging 1 mile and about 1,200 feet down the canyon wall. Along this segment, fall color is noncommittal, relegating itself to errant patches on distant peaks and slopes.

At about mile 1.75, you pass the Stradling Canyon Trail and, a bit farther, the Cinch Hook Butte Trail. The fall color begins as **boxelder** trees start to make appearances, along with the rosy tints of **poison ivy**, in canyon crooks. **Canyon grape** drapes gold strands of maplelike leaves down slopes and pine trees.

Once the trail hits the canyon floor, Pine Canyon becomes the epitome of a storybook chasm. Pine Creek creates a moist environment that nourishes a cover of pines and colorful hardwoods; moss wraps around boulders, and fern-covered, dripping springs seep into glass-clear pools. The flame of creek side **bigtooth maple, boxelder,** and **cottonwood** trees flickers from yellow to scarlet red with a blush of russet from **Gambel oak** trees in between. Look for signs pointing out areas of interest along the creek, such as Tiny Cave and Dripping Springs.

When the trail parts from the creek about 3 miles from the trailhead, **Gambel oak** trees provide most of the color in the drier pine-oak vegetation. This spot makes for a good turnaround point for a day hike. The trail

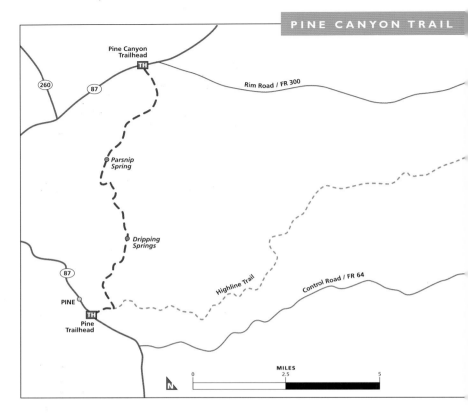

meanders in and out of shallow canyons as it contours the south side of the Rim. Along the way, you can see the hamlet of Pine, cozy as a sleepy hollow, from points along the trail.

After passing muddy Dripping Springs, which coaxes a bit of fall color from **New Mexico locust** trees, the trail continues another 1.5 miles to the Highline Trail along an exposed track, then on to the Pine Trailhead, a total of 8 miles. This makes a good shuttle hike, but a round-trip hike is quite comfortable for seasoned hikers.

Horton Creek Loop

Larry Ulrich

TRAIL RATING	moderate
TRAIL LENGTH	10-mile loop
LOCATION	Payson
ELEVATION	5,400–6,800 feet
CONTACT	Tonto National Forest, 520-474-7900
PEAK COLOR	mid-October
DIRECTIONS	From Payson, take Arizona 260 east 15.8 miles and turn north (left) onto FR 289. Drive 0.8 mile to the parking area across from Upper Tonto Campground. Cross the road and enter the campground to get to the trail.

Dropping immediately in and out of the Horton Creek drainage, the trail starts out with a show of color from **Fremont cottonwood** and **Gambel oak** trees. Because the trail, which starts on an old wagon road, never strays far from the drainage, **canyon grape** and **Virginia creeper** are colorful companions, adding gold and scarlet colors to the hike. When the trail comes to a fork, veer right to stay near the creek and pass through a gate into a series of strawed meadows colored by colonies of purpled **sumac**.

You'll see footpaths branching from the trail that lead to the creek banks where anglers often fish for trout. Along the creek, **Arizona sycamore**, **Arizona walnut**, and **boxelder** trees toss tan and golden reflections onto the pools of water.

When the trail saddles up to the creek, giant **Arizona sycamore** trees, with their mottled trunks and gnarly limbs, canopy the banks on one side; **thinleaf alder** trees line up on the other, while mixed conifers hang in the background. From here, the trail climbs out of the drainage and returns to the old wagon road and clambers through a ponderosa pine forest.

With the trail just within earshot of the creek, you can still see stitches of fall color woven through the pines. **Gambel oak** trees, with **canyon grape** dangling from their limbs, border the trail as it picks through a steep, rocky grade. **Virginia creeper** and **Arizona sycamore** color a drainage that the trail dips into just before it meets up with the creek again at about mile 2. When you notice a particularly large cascade pouring over a ledge of sandstone, look for a fluorescent flame of **bigtooth maple** trees.

The creek banks become a riot of color with shades of gold, red, salmon, and peach until the trail comes to a heap of boulders and parts company with the

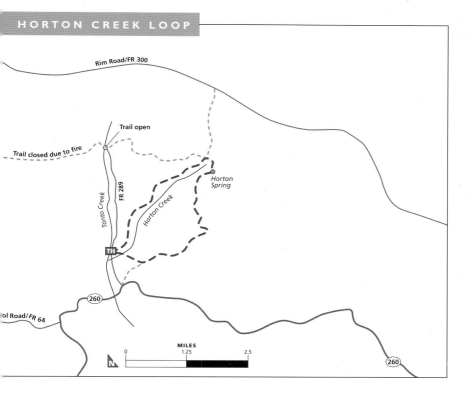

HORTON CREEK LOOP

Rim Road/FR 300

Trail open

Trail closed due to fire

Horton
Spring

Tonto Creek

FR 289

Horton Creek

TH

260

ol Road/FR 64

MILES
0   1.25   2.5

N

260

waterway. The trail heads back into the pines, but stays within a glance of the fall color.

When the trail comes to another fork, you can take either path. The left path, which is the maintained trail, continues on an uphill slog that cuts through ponderosa pines. The trail to the right is an unmaintained path that climbs along a maple-lined section of creek with cascades that bounce down moss-covered rocks. Though the more beautiful of the two choices, this path requires good route-finding skills.

Both paths lead up to the Highline Trail and the creek's genesis at Horton Springs. Before crossing the creek and continuing on the Highline Trail, take a moment to see where the springs gush out of the side of the Mogollon Rim. For a shorter day hike, this makes a good turnaround point.

Once across the creek, the trail switchbacks up a ridge where you catch a quick glimpse of the rim's spired limestone ledge just before the trail heads down the other side. Rock-ribbed and steep, the trail drops through the sweet-smelling pines and heads to another drainage where **boxelder**, **Gambel oak**, and **bigtooth maple** trees hang out.

Fall colors wrap around the trail as it parallels the drainage, and when it turns away to climb to the top of the rim, the **bigtooth maple** trees follow.

SUMAC
Rhus glabra

One of the first trees to change in the fall, sumac has leaves that feature a range of colors from yellow to maroon with orange and red in between. The trees can grow up to 20 feet high, but usually reach half that height.

The fruit, which looks like a cluster of red velvet berries, feeds more than 30 species of birds. Humans like the fruit, too. The berries, tart with malic acid, make a beverage reminiscent of lemonade. To make sumac lemonade according to one recipe: "Separate any questionable fruit from a lavish handful of the mature red berries, mash the remainder just enough to break the skins, cover with bubbling water, and move from the heat to steep until the beverage is well colored. Strain through fine cloth to remove the fine hairs. Then sweeten to taste and serve hot or cold." The berries are best gathered in late summer or early fall.

Herbalists use the berries, bark, and leaves for urinary tract problems and inflammation. Some American Indians used a wet dressing of the leaves and fruit to relieve discomfort from poison ivy. American Indians also used the leaves to make kinnikinnick, a mixture of herbs used as a tobacco substitute.

At rim top, you see exceptional views where clearings allow quick glances of the rim's layout and surrounding mountains.

The trail starts on a diagonal path down the rim, rising and falling over ridges. **Gambel oak** and ponderosa pine trees dominate, except in ravines where **bigtooth maple** trees flare red. The trail eventually drops into the Supai formation, where the fall color is replaced by strata of red rock the same as in Sedona.

At about mile 7.5, the trail comes to an intersection. Veer right onto the Derrick Trail, a 2.5 mile downhill hike back to the Upper Tonto Campground. Once you reach the campground, turn left and follow the road back to the parking area.

See Canyon Trail

Larry Ulrich

TRAIL RATING	difficult
TRAIL LENGTH	3.75 miles one way
LOCATION	Payson
ELEVATION	6,100–7,860 feet
CONTACT	Tonto National Forest, 520-474-7900
PEAK COLOR	mid-October
DIRECTIONS	From Payson, drive east on Arizona 260 about 21 miles to FR 284. Turn north (left) and drive 1.6 miles to the trailhead.

See Canyon, named for Charley and John See, the father and son who settled there around 1900, is famous for some of the best fall color on the Mogollon Rim. The trail offers early hints of its wealth of color when it begins in a forest of pine and **bigtooth maple** trees that cover the path down to the banks of Christopher Creek a short distance away.

At the creek, the trail divulges most of the color-producing trees — **boxelder**, **bigtooth maple**, **velvet ash**, and **Gambel oak** — found along the rest of its course as it climbs to the top of the Mogollon Rim. Along the creek banks, watch for colonies of **agrimonia**, a wildflower in the rose family, that paint the ground in shades of yellow, and look for the gold streamers of **canyon grape** dripping from trees.

But this early color is only a taste, as the trail quickly exits the drainage and enters an evergreen wooded area that parallels the creek. The trail keeps close enough to the drainage to keep sight of the palette of color the creek hosts along its banks. When you come to a signed fork, veer left.

Just over 0.5 mile, the color disappears temporarily as the trail distances itself from the creek and starts its rigorous climb up the Mogollon rim. The outflow from See Spring, at about mile 1, coaxes the color back to the trail. The path starts to flame with **bigtooth maple** trees when it makes its way back to the creek and resumes its first of several creek crossings.

By mile 1.5, a mosaic of colors becomes your constant companion as the trail sticks close to the creek drainage for the remainder of the hike, passing through thick covers of **bigtooth maples**. At this point, the trail becomes austere in its travel to the top. Trail washouts appear, and the grade has intensely steep moments. One particularly confusing washout occurs at mile 2.5. Cairns indicate routes on both sides of the drainage. For the easier,

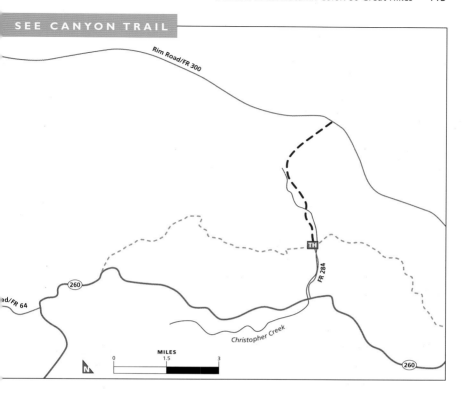

SEE CANYON TRAIL

but still challenging, route, cross the rock-ribbed creek bed and continue on the left side of the drainage.

The color you experience on this maple-rich section may vary considerably. Some trees will stick to yellow hues, especially in shadier areas. Coral, brick red, and scarlet leaves glow in sunlit sections. Some trees might feature mottles of color, their treetops turned while the rest of the branches remain a summery green. And some trees are lit up like Christmas next to others that haven't a clue. Like temperamental artists that won't perform except under ideal conditions, fall colors keep capricious schedules.

At mile 3.25, the **bigtooth maple** trees relinquish their hold on the path to a forest of mixed conifers. Stands of **aspens** glow among the evergreens covering the canyon wall.

The last 0.5 mile of the trail continues up a rocky slope that finally ends at FR 300. Return the way you came.

Autumn
Hike 29 *Pine Mountain Loop*

TRAIL RATING	moderate
TRAIL LENGTH	9.6-mile loop
LOCATION	Salt Flat Trailhead, Pine Mountain Wilderness
ELEVATION	5,200–6,814 feet
CONTACT	Prescott National Forest, 520-567-4121
PEAK COLOR	end of October
SPECIAL ONSIDERATIONS	No mechanized equipment, including bicycles, is allowed in the Pine Mountain Wilderness.
DIRECTIONS	From Phoenix, take Interstate 17 north about 53 miles to the Dugas interchange (Exit 268). Go east (right) on Dugas Road to the town of Dugas, and then follow FR 68 about 9 miles to the trailhead. The drive, which requires a high-clearance vehicle, will take about an hour.

Starting out in a riparian forest along Sycamore Creek on the Nelson Trail, this loop hike eventually climbs 1,500 feet up to the Verde Rim as it aims for its high point atop Pine Mountain. The gathering of **Arizona walnut**, **Arizona sycamore**, and **Gambel oak** trees at the trail's start weaves a cool cover of shade in the summer, then turns into a gold and russet canopy in the fall.

The trail follows Sycamore Creek, where trout break the ice-cold water's surface and fallen **Arizona sycamore** leaves steeping along the soggy banks release a spicy-sweet aroma. Hawks squawk in the treetops lining the creek, and bear signs, fresh enough to evoke caution, often blaze the trail. An apple orchard at the Nelson Place, a homestead eroded down to a stone wall located in the first mile of the hike, draws the bruins. Elk, mountain lion, and deer also share the wilderness.

Shortly after the trail squishes through the spongy, spring-fed ground at the Nelson Place, it enters the Pine Mountain Wilderness. The path separates from Sycamore Creek and starts to climb up to the Verde Rim. Ponderosa pine and **Gambel oak** trees provide immediate shade, and within 1 mile **bigtooth maple** trees make a surprise staccato appearance along the steep slopes of the drainage. An anomalous stand of **aspen** trees waits in a crevice near the top of the rim.

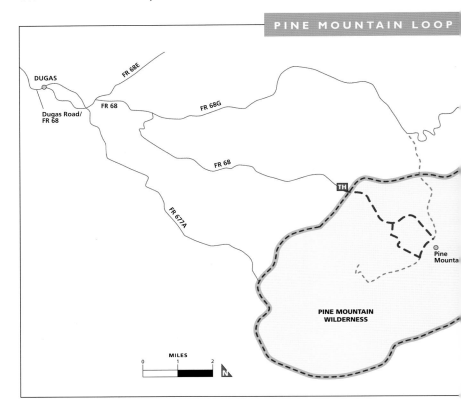

At the Verde Rim Trail, mile 4.3, turn right and head toward Pine Mountain. In about 0.33 mile, an ancillary footpath takes you to the top of the mountain for a 360-degree panorama of Horseshoe Lake to the south, the rugged Mogollon Rim to the east, the Verde Valley to the north, and the Bradshaw Mountains to the west. In late fall, stands of **Fremont cottonwood** trees in the valley glow golden.

At mile 5.2, turn right onto the Pine Mountain Trail and zigzag 1.2 miles down the mountain through **Gambel oak** groves back to the Nelson Trail. Turn left onto the Nelson Trail and retrace your earlier steps another 3.2 miles back to the trailhead.

Cave Creek Trail

TRAIL RATING	moderate
TRAIL LENGTH	4–10 miles one way
LOCATION	Phoenix
ELEVATION	2,600–3,440 feet
CONTACT	Tonto National Forest, 480-595-3300
PEAK COLOR	late November
DIRECTIONS	From Phoenix, take Cave Creek Road northeast to its end at FR 24. Continue north on FR 24 about 9 miles to the Seven Springs Recreation Area. Pull into the signed trailhead lot on the west side of the road.

Fall colors linger awhile in the lower desert elevations, and you may get your last glimpse of them on this trail that straddles Cave Creek. The trail starts just north of the Seven Springs Campground, built in the 1930s by the Civilian Conservation Corps, a Depression-era work relief program. The campground, surrounded by a riparian cover of **Arizona sycamore**, **velvet ash**, and **Fremont cottonwood** trees, creates an oasis atmosphere in the middle of the desert. This atmosphere joins you on the trail as it follows Cave Creek through an Upper Sonoran Desert life zone.

After traveling south 0.5 mile, the trail crosses FR 24B, drops into the creek drainage, then veers right to parallel the creek. **Arizona sycamore** trees emanate an orange hue from a rock-ribbed delta along the banks of the creek and dominate the fall color in the creek drainage. When the trail intersects with the Cottonwood Trail, continue straight on the Cave Creek Trail.

Fremont cottonwood, **velvet ash**, and **willow** trees join the **Arizona sycamore** trees in producing a vibrant golden glow near the trail. Right along the trail, juniper trees, blue-green buckthorn bushes, scrub oak, and catclaw prevail.

At mile 1, you'll notice that the **Arizona sycamore** trees triple in size and number. Huddled on an island delta where the creek forks, the forest indicates the surrounding abundant supply of water. The **Arizona sycamore's** mottled white trunks reflect in the emerald water filled with pockets of their honey-colored leaves.

With the more consistent supply of moisture in this specific area, hearty **velvet ash** trees canopy the trail and **canyon grape** wraps around bushes and

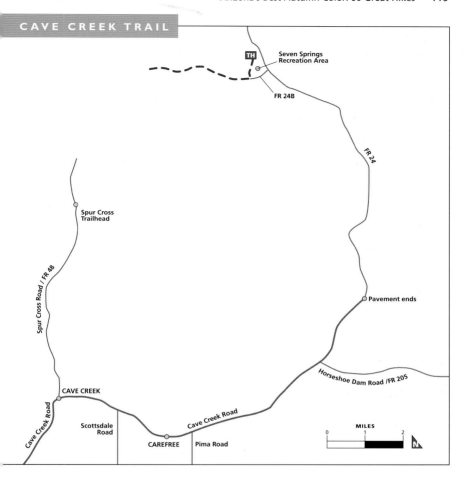

CAVE CREEK TRAIL

hangs from trees. **Arizona sycamore** trees hop the creek and join the **velvet ash** and juniper trees along the trail.

Within 0.25 mile, the riparian cover separates to show the surrounding peaks. Unlike the lushness of the creek banks, these hillsides have a cover of scrubby desert vegetation such as mesquite trees, catclaw, prickly pear and cholla cactus, juniper trees, and scrub oak.

The trail passes through a green metal gate, then drops into the drainage next to a golden wall of **willow** trees at about mile 2. Immediately, the trail rock hops across the creek and picks through a rocky delta into the shady cover of **velvet ash** and **Arizona sycamore** trees. Pastel-leaved **skunkbush** makes a brief appearance.

With the trail now on the south side of the canyon, you can see saguaro cacti running up the sun-drenched northern slopes. Just before the trail passes a primitive camp on a grassy bench, look for a rare, crested saguaro on the north canyon wall.

The crested—or cristate—saguaros have fan-shaped crowns. Instead of branching arms, like normal saguaros, the growing tips deviate into a filigree shape. Some botanists think a genetic quirk causes the anomalous growth pattern; others think frost or lightning causes it. Approximately one of every 200,000 saguaros is crested.

After climbing a couple hundred feet above the drainage, the trail looks down on the treetops of **Arizona sycamores** and islands of gray boulders in the creek bed for the next 0.5 mile. At mile 2.8, the trail drops into the drainage, hops briefly across the creek, then climbs back above the creek on the north canyon wall where rust-colored outcroppings encroach and saguaro cacti file past. Below, a thick array of **velvet ash**, **Fremont cottonwood**, and **willow** trees paint the creek banks gold. In about 0.25 mile, watch for a footpath that drops into the drainage to a double cascade pouring through a jumble of boulders.

The trail continues for another 0.75 mile to the intersection with the Skunk Tank Trail. From here, you can continue 6 miles on the Cave Creek Trail; continue on the Skunk Tank, Quien Sabe, and Cottonwood Trails for a 10-mile loop; or return the way you came.

ARIZONA SYCAMORE

Platanus wrightii

Arizona sycamore trees lend a poetic ambience to any forest. Their white or pale green mottled bark, limbs that point like craggy fingers, and spicy-sweet aroma create an attractive display. In the fall, their trident leaves turn the color of honey.

Arizona sycamore trees flourish around water. When you see them, you know a perennial source of water lies nearby. The more consistent the water source, the more sumptuous the sycamores.

Fish Creek Canyon

TRAIL RATING	difficult
TRAIL LENGTH	1 mile one way
LOCATION	Apache Junction
ELEVATION	2,200 feet
CONTACT	Tonto National Forest, 480-610-3300
PEAK COLOR	late November
SPECIAL CONSIDERATIONS	This route is not a designated wilderness system trail, and it is never maintained.
DIRECTIONS	From Apache Junction, go northeast on Arizona 88, past Tortilla Flat, about 22 miles to the bridge at Fish Creek. Park on the east side of the bridge.

When President Theodore Roosevelt toured the Apache Trail, the road that winds along the north side of the Superstition Mountains, he compared the view of Fish Creek Canyon with the magnificence of the Grand Canyon. The deep canyon, with its precipitous stratified walls, makes an exquisite panoramic scene from the road.

But, much like the Grand Canyon, a different world awaits on the canyon floor. A crystal stream during wet weather, raspy boulders, volcanic tuff peaks, and lush riparian cover surrounded by Sonoran desert vegetation make for a fascinating hike. Add the golden glow of fall color, and you have one of the best fall color hikes in central Arizona.

The hike starts on the west side of the bridge that crosses Fish Creek, on a footpath that scrambles up the western wall of Fish Creek Canyon. When you have a choice, take the higher trail up to a yawn of an alcove, then follow the path as it drops to the canyon floor.

Right away, you're in the center of a rich display of color created by **velvet ash, willow, Fremont cottonwood,** and **Arizona walnut** trees. **Arizona sycamore** trees pepper the golden array with their tan leaves.

The canyon walls display a variety of textures and colors. Volcanic tuff emanates a golden hue, especially on the upper walls looming several hundred feet above the floor. A meld of volcanic rock and conglomerate produces a surface full of dents, pocks, spires, and alcoves. Arches let in shafts of daylight.

Closer to the stream, the walls are chewed by erosion and stuffed with fall color. Trees vault between boulders, climb up sloping benches, and wedge between walls. **Canyon grape** clings to bushes and trees nestled in the canyon

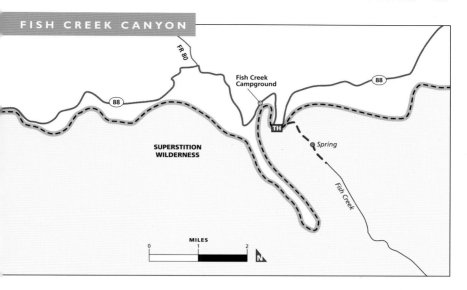

wall. In wet weather, cold mountain water rushes over a mosaic of river rocks, past pools cluttered with collections of colored leaves. **Arizona sycamore** leaves release a sweet pungency as they steep in the moist environment.

The trek through the canyon proceeds without a trail. Once in a while, a beaten path negotiates a route around a pool or up an outcropping, but for the most part, the hike requires rock hops and scrambles. Take your time, enjoy the rocks and autumn color, spend a moment watching the cascades pour into deep pools, and stop to explore benches for scenic vantage points—such as the one at mile 0.5.

At this particular bench, saguaro cacti gather on the east wall above the bench and peer into the canyon, reminding you that this lush environment cuts through a sere desert. The prickly cactus forest dodges spires and peaks on the canyon wall, which is streaked with charcoal water marks.

Just below the bench, truck-sized boulders lie pell-mell in the gorge, making the going slow for the next 0.25 mile. Then the canyon opens up slightly and allows for a comfortable scramble. After another 0.25 mile, the vegetation turns to thickets and hiking becomes more difficult. Because of this, mile 1 makes a good turnaround point. Return the way you came.

Six Shooter Trail

TRAIL RATING	strenuous
TRAIL LENGTH	6 miles one way
LOCATION	Globe
ELEVATION	4,320–7,680 feet
CONTACT	Tonto National Forest, 520-425-7189
PEAK COLOR	mid- to late October
SPECIAL CONSIDERATIONS	This trail is not suitable for equestrian use.
DIRECTIONS	From the western edge of Globe on US 60, drive east through the town and turn south (right) on Hill Street just past mile marker 251. Follow the brown and white signs to the Pinal Mountain Recreation Area for 1.2 miles and turn right onto Ice House Canyon Road. Drive 1.8 miles to a stop sign and continue straight to the end of the pavement. Drive 0.5 mile to the CCC Camp picnic area and the Six Shooter Trailhead.

It is not often that you come across a trail with an identity crisis. The phenomenon occurs mostly on sky islands—mountains that rise sharply from the desert floor—where pine, riparian, desert, and mixed conifer communities cross each other indiscriminately. The tangled biomes produce an eclectic blend of diversity and beauty that makes for great vegetation visuals.

Because the Six Shooter Trail climbs a sky island, it takes on the mountain's manic personality. Within 6 miles and an almost 3,000-foot elevation change, the trail transports you from scrubby chaparral mix along mountain slopes to quaking **aspen** trees at its end near Ferndell Spring. In between, it deviates between high-country pines, New England–style forests, and classic high desert vegetation.

The trail's first mile is in the heat of the sun among manzanita bushes until it drops into the Six Shooter Creek drainage. **Arizona sycamore, hackberry,** and **Fremont cottonwood** trees line the creek banks, showing off golden- and honey-colored leaves. The trail climbs out of the oasis quickly, heading back into the chaparral as it makes a steady ascent up the mountain. Along the way, you see panoramic views of the Globe-Miami area.

By mile 2, the trail ducks under canopies of **Gambel oak** trees, where fall paints golds and russets on their leaves. In another mile, depending on which side of the canyon it's on, the trail deviates from a rugged trek through a high desert mix of agave, piñon, juniper, and cactus nestled on rocky outcroppings to a cool climb through a cover of mixed pines and **Gambel oak** trees. **Aspen** and **Arizona walnut** trees pour splashes of gold into moist crooks of the trail at creek crossings.

ARIZONA WALNUT

Juglans major

In the fall, the Arizona walnut tree's lance-shaped serrated leaflets transform from their yellowish-green color to gold. If you pluck a leaf and crush it, you'll notice a distinctive spicy odor and the yellow juice will stain your hand. The juice from walnut leaves and hulls is used as a natural dye.

The juice was once popular among pioneers and American Indians for getting rid of lice, intestinal worms, and bedbugs. This is not surprising when you consider that walnuts contain the chemical juglone, which pharmacognosist Albert Leung, Ph.D., says helps treat mite infestations. In Turkish folk medicine, husks were used for glandular problems—another sensible remedy when you consider a decoction of green walnuts boosts thyroxine levels by at least 30 percent.

Some American Indians made a decoction of the bark as an external wash for arthritis. In the fall, pioneers gathered the inner bark of the root to use as a remedy when one felt "liverish."

The trees bloom in May and produce fruit in the fall. If you take the time to dig the nutmeats out of their complicated hulls, you'll find their sweetness worth the effort.

Still climbing, the trail pulls away from the canyon's crevice and enters a pine-oak forest around mile 4. Granite boulders loll around the forest floor, tawny from pine needles and crisped oak leaves. In the right weather conditions of frostless nights and sunny days, the oaks produce a rich golden glow.

Sometimes, while passing through this forested section, you'll see clues of black bear grubbing along the trail where smaller granite boulders lie overturned. Bobcat, white-tailed deer, mountain lion, and coatimundi also roam the mountain.

At mile 4.5, the trail joins an old road surrounded by a forest of hardwoods and mixed conifers, and **bigtooth maple** and **velvet ash** trees come on the scene. The trail then abruptly descends several hundred feet and

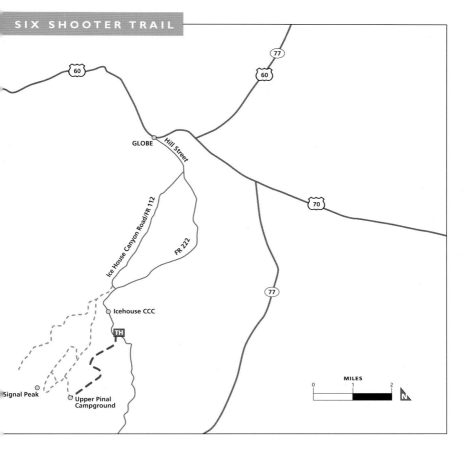

levels off until it reaches a mine shaft. In the 1880s, the working mine sat opposite a sawmill and cabin. One historic account says that the workers at the sawmill all seemed to pack six-shooters, which is how the canyon got its name.

The mine eventually flooded with water and the forest was razed by overharvesting of timber. Now, the trees have recouped and a shock of grass follows the trickle of water from the mine across the black-dirt trail to the skeletal remains of the mill and cabin.

The trail takes to climbing again and struggles another mile toward Ferndell Spring. At about mile 5.5, the trail veers off the road onto a single track on the right, entering a forest that resembles a Canadian life zone full of mixed conifers and **aspen** trees. The trail ends about 0.25 mile beyond Ferndell Spring at its junction with the Middle Trail just short of the top of Pinal Mountain, which is crowned with golden **aspen** trees. Return the way you came.

Bonita Creek

TRAIL RATING	moderate
TRAIL LENGTH	3.5 miles or more one way
LOCATION	Safford
ELEVATION	3,100 feet
CONTACT	Bureau of Land Management, 520-348-4400
PEAK COLOR	mid-November
SPECIAL CONSIDERATIONS	Practicing Leave No Trace ethics is essential around this creek's pristine environment. Watch for flash floods in wet weather. This creek hike has no maintained trail.
DIRECTIONS	From Safford, drive east on US 70. From mile marker 341, go 3.3 miles and turn north (left) onto Sanchez Road. Drive 12.5 miles, following signs, to West Bonita Rim Road, then go 1.7 miles, veer right over the cattle guard, and continue straight for 3.2 miles. At Red Knolls Canyon Road, veer right and go 3.6 miles to the creek. The drive will take more than an hour-and-a-half and requires a four-wheel-drive vehicle.

Located in the Gila Box Riparian National Conservation Area, one of the most significant riparian zones in the Southwest, Bonita Creek is known for its exceptional water quality. The rich riparian waterway provides habitat for five species of native fish, more than 200 species of Neotropical migratory birds, and several big game animals such as Rocky Mountain bighorn sheep, bear, javelina, and mule deer. If the color lingers into December, you may spot a bald eagle or peregrine falcon on its way southward.

Situated between erratically eroded volcanic cliffs melded with Gila conglomerate, Bonita Creek makes an extraordinarily scenic hike. In the fall, its riparian cover provides a golden corridor of color when **Fremont cottonwood**, **willow**, **velvet ash**, **Arizona walnut**, and **Arizona sycamore** trees turn bright gold.

The trailless canyon route often allows you to follow the creek along its banks. However, you can expect to cross and wade through the creek repeatedly. Occasionally, the route demands bushwhacking around beaver dams (at mile 1.5) and outcroppings in the Narrows (that start at mile 1 and continue to mile 3.25) just below Midnight Canyon.

As a good water source located in the middle of nowhere, the creek drew a colorful meld of outlaws, roughnecks, and loners who spanned cultures from Chinese and Anglos to Mexicans and Apaches. Homesteads once lined the creek banks, and you might see remnants of old buildings built right into the canyon walls or deteriorated in mesquite bosquets. The Anasazi also used to live in areas along the creek, and you can see their cliff dwellings along your hike.

You can anticipate traveling about 1 mile per hour in the canyon. With that in mind, Midnight Canyon, at about mile 3.5, makes a good turnaround point.

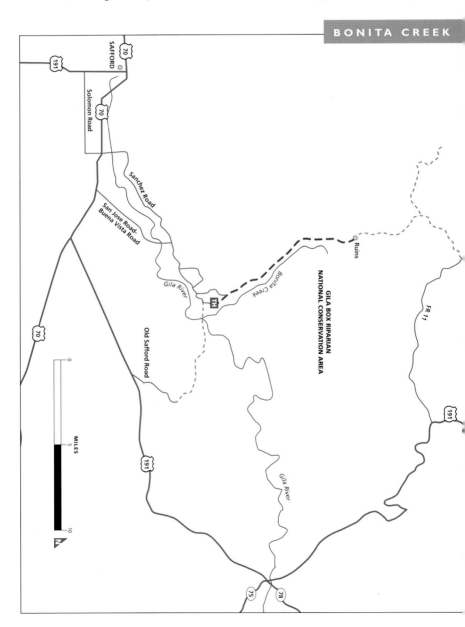

BONITA CREEK

Bear Wallow Loop

Larry Ulrich

TRAIL RATING	strenuous
TRAIL LENGTH	7 mile loop
LOCATION	Alpine
ELEVATION	8,800—7,768 feet
CONTACT	Apache-Sitgreaves National Forest, 520-339-4384
PEAK COLOR	end of September to beginning of October
SPECIAL CONSIDERATIONS	The trail is located in the Bear Wallow Wilderness, where no mechanized vehicles, including mountain bikes, are allowed.
DIRECTIONS	From Alpine, at the intersection of US Highways 180 and 191, drive south on US 191 for about 22 miles to Hannagan Meadow. From Hannagan Meadow, drive another 5 miles south on US 191 to FR 25 and turn west (right). Drive about 3 miles to the trailhead on the left.

Bear wallows were common in this drainage when rancher Pete Slaughter drove cattle through it in the late 1800s. The bears liked to laze in the wallows to escape the biting flies. Along this hike, there's still a good chance you might see a black bear as well as an elk, mountain lion, or even a Mexican gray wolf. The remote drainage, with its perennial water source, makes an attractive habitat for the animals, and the fall color adds an attraction for humans.

Aspen trees supply most of the color on this loop trail, and you first see them at about 0.5 mile as the trail descends the north fork of Bear Wallow Creek into the Bear Wallow Wilderness. About mile 1, watch for a handful of **Rocky Mountain maple** trees in the drainage next to the trail. Though not as bold in color as **bigtooth maple** trees, these trees may add a blush of red to the yellow glow of surrounding **New Mexico locust** trees, **wild rose** bushes, and **canyon grape**.

By mile 1.5, the trail steps onto the floor of the Bear Wallow drainage. Stands of **aspen** sprawl across the canyon slopes, and the trail brushes past handfuls of **aspen** as they mingle with mixed conifers scattered on the canyon floor. As the trail's elevation declines, the **aspen** trees leave the meadows and keep to the canyon walls.

At mile 2.6, the trail intersects with the Reno Trail, your path back up to the rim. However, you can hike 0.25 mile farther on the trail (which travels 5 more miles to the San Carlos Indian Reservation) to Bear Wallow Creek, where a moister environment supports a stand of **aspen** that crowds around the creek near the canyon's north face. The environment also encourages **poison ivy**, which adds a flame of color, too.

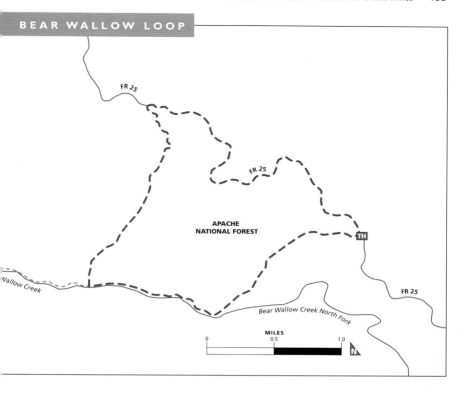

If you hike to Bear Wallow Creek, backtrack to the Reno Trail to continue on the loop hike. This section of the loop climbs about 1,600 feet in 1.9 miles.

Within 0.5 mile, the trail enters a stand of **aspen** in the predominately ponderosa pine forest. And even though the **aspen** trees don't reappear until the upper half of the trail, they do favor the other side of the canyon where you can see them glowing across the whole upper canyon wall for the rest of the hike.

In the meantime, it's a steep slog up the canyon through the pines. By mile 3.6, the **aspen** trees reappear and surround the trail for the rest of its climb up to the rim where more stands await.

For the last leg of the loop, turn right onto FR 25. The road, lined with **aspen** trees, evokes an exquisite fall atmosphere with its strong display of color. Follow the road 2.5 miles back to the Bear Wallow Trailhead.

Autumn
Hike 35

Escudilla National Recreation Trail

TRAIL RATING	strenuous
TRAIL LENGTH	3.0 miles one way
LOCATION	Escudilla Mountain Wilderness
ELEVATION	9,480–10,876 feet
CONTACT	Apache-Sitgreaves National Forest, 520-339-4384
PEAK COLOR	end of September to beginning of October
SPECIAL CONSIDERATIONS	This trail is in the Escudilla Mountain Wilderness, where no mechanized vehicles, including mountain bikes, are allowed.
DIRECTIONS	From Eagar, drive 21.5 miles south on US 180/191 and, about 3 miles past Nutrioso, turn east (left) onto FR 56. Drive 4.9 miles to the trailhead, veering left at the Terry Flat Loop sign.

Thanks to a forest fire in 1951, some of Arizona's best **aspen** color spreads across the peaks of the Escudilla Mountain Wilderness. The fire wiped out the mixed conifer growth on the mountain, making way for nature's cycle of filling in the open space with stands of **aspen** trees.

The Escudilla National Recreation Trail starts off in the thick of color and brings you through its craterlike bowl where stands of mixed conifers and **aspen** trees tread across alpine meadows. (The bowl inspired the trail's name, Escudilla, which is Spanish for "large bowl.") The trail then climbs to the top of Escudilla Mountain to show you a dramatic spread of color for miles around.

The trail parallels Profanity Ridge, named by local people who slogged up the steep ridge day after day to fight the fire in 1951. The trail starts its uphill grind in a burst of gold as it enters a dense **aspen** forest. The glow from the **aspen** leaves becomes so intense that you feel as if you're walking in a golden cavern. The surrounding slopes—if you could see them from the trail's corridor through the color—glow gold from nonstop stands of **aspen** trees.

Within 0.5 mile, the **aspen** trees decrease in height, allowing dapples of sunlight to enhance their glimmer. In another 0.25 mile, meadows—now strawed from frosts—open around the trail. Islands of dark green firs and spruce mingled with **aspen** make a stunning sight in the flaxen sea of grass.

At mile 1.5, you get a reprieve from the trail's steep slog when it crests a ridge and experiences a bit of downhill in a fir-spruce forest. When it reaches another meadow, the trail continues its climb over another ridge, then relaxes once again through another spruce-fir forest glinting with gold from small stands of **aspen** mixed with the conifers.

The trail heaves up the final 0.25 mile to a fire tower where you can see a patchwork of gold and green on the surrounding peaks and slopes. On a clear day, you can see New Mexico to the east, sacred Mt. Baldy to the west, the San Francisco Peaks to the northwest, and the Pinal Mountains to the southwest.

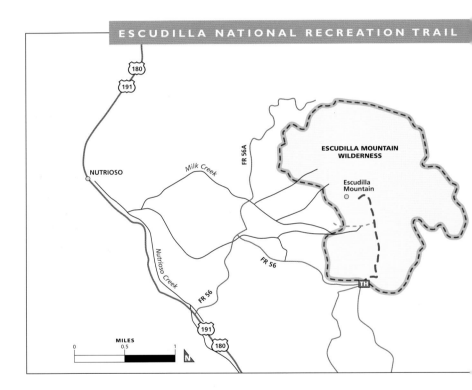

*Besides aspen groves, the Escudilla Mountain Wilderness also encompasses
steep ridges, meadows, and fir-spruce forests, along with great views.*

KP Creek Trail

Larry Ulrich

During its 9.4 miles to the Steeple Trail, the KP Creek Trail takes you
through a variety of biomes in the Blue Range Primitive Area—from
an alpine atmosphere to high desert mountaintops and riparian rambles. A
short day hike to the confluence of the south and north forks of the creek
brings you through a wild and remote environment painted in fall colors
ranging from flamingo to scarlet to shimmering gold.

At its start, the KP Creek Trail crosses an alpine meadow ringed by fir
and spruce trees before it enters a wooded canyon. The trail follows the South
Fork of KP Creek as it tumbles about 3 miles and 1,160 feet to the creek's
North Fork. The two forks combine to form KP Creek, which flows south-
eastward to join the Blue River.

Mixed conifers surround the trail where it enters the forest on the north
slope of the drainage high above the South Fork. **Aspen** trees watch from a

TRAIL RATING	strenuous
TRAIL LENGTH	3 miles one way
LOCATION	Alpine
ELEVATION	8,960–7,800 feet
CONTACT	Apache-Sitgreaves National Forest, 520-339-4384
PEAK COLOR	end of September to beginning of October
DIRECTIONS	From Alpine, take US 191 south about 28 miles and turn east (left) at the signed road leading to KP Campground. Drive 1.2 miles to the trailhead.

KP CREEK TRAIL

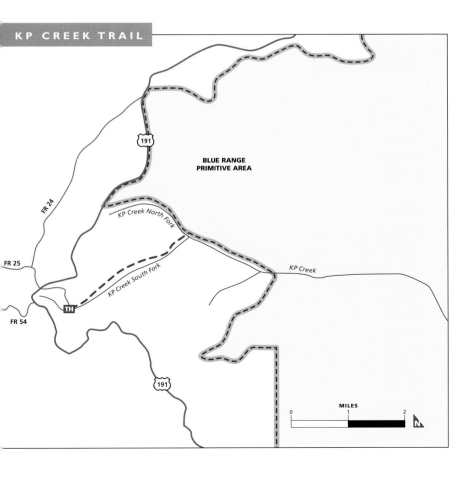

distance. This alpine forest is prime spotted owl habitat, and you may see one of the brown and white raptors flapping below the treetops or hear its doglike barks and cries.

As the trail descends into the drainage, the **aspen** trees move closer, edging right along the path. **Rocky Mountain maple** and **Gambel oak** trees mix together, embroidering the upper slope with hues of gold and red. Then the trees jump the trail into moist crooks, coloring both sides of the path.

At mile 1, the trail starts to switchback deeper into the canyon. As it does, you see views of the canyon's south wall, now glittering gold from the forest of **aspen** trees blanketing the whole slope. When the trail finally lands on the canyon floor, it places you right next to the South Fork. **Rocky Mountain maple** trees immediately crowd around the stream, but the **aspen** trees hang back on the upper walls for a while, then suddenly approach the trail after it passes through a small meadow and starts to drop toward KP Creek. **Gambel oak** trees join the **aspen** later and become especially prominent around an outcropping on the right that butts up to the trail.

The trail climbs briefly out of the drainage, crosses a sunny hillside, and drops again into the drainage. Instead of crossing the creek to continue on the KP Creek Trail, make a hairpin right turn on a beaten path, which takes you to a pretty cascade on the North Fork and then to the confluence. The confluence shows a particularly brilliant display of color with gold leaves of **willows**, rosy hues of **red-osier dogwood**, and hints of red from **Rocky Mountain maple** trees. Return the way you came.

Lanphier Trail

Larry Ulrich

Tucked in the folds of the remote Blue Range Primitive Area, Lanphier Canyon makes a wild and colorful environment for a hike. A corral marks the beginning of the hike, which starts on the Largo Canyon Trail. In the distance, streamside **velvet ash**, **Gambel oak**, **Arizona walnut**, and **boxelder** trees in Lanphier Canyon's bottom supply a constant glow of gold color as the trail climbs up to the top of a ridge about 0.5 mile away.

As the trail drops over the ridge top, veer left onto the Lanphier Trail. The trail parallels Lanphier Creek for the next 2.6 miles, passing a vivid demonstration of how colorful fall can get in mountain canyons: **Gambel oak** trees sprawl across the path, and **velvet ash** and **Arizona walnut** trees crowd around the creek. The russet and gold colors brighten up the dark chasm. **Canyon grape** twines itself everywhere, robing even the most lackluster trees in gold. Patches of **poison ivy** ruddy the ground.

When the trail gets close enough to peer into the creek, watch for scarlet-colored **Virginia creeper**, one of the first botanicals to turn color in the fall.

TRAIL RATING	strenuous
TRAIL LENGTH	5.6 miles one way
LOCATION	Blue Range Primitive Area
ELEVATION	5,600–7,360 feet
CONTACT	Apache-Sitgreaves National Forest, 520-339-4384
PEAK COLOR	mid-October
SPECIAL CONSIDERATIONS	No mechanized vehicles, including mountain bikes, are allowed on the trail.
DIRECTIONS	From Alpine, drive about 3 miles east on US 180 and turn south (right) onto Blue River Road (FR 281). Drive about 25 miles to the Blue Administration Site and a trailhead marked Largo and Foote Creek Trailhead. Walk to the right of the trailhead poster board through two gates to the Blue River. Cross the river and head to a corral, which marks the beginning of the trail.

VIRGINIA CREEPER

Parthenocissus inserta

Part of the grape family, Virginia creeper coils and drapes up trees and rockwalls like its relative, canyon grape. The palmate leaves of Virginia creeper turn a brilliant scarlet color, as opposed to canyon grape's maple-shaped gold. Virginia creeper vines are the first vines to blush during the fall.

The vines prefer moist canyons and roadsides. A perennial water source and adequate shadows make a comfortable environment for Virginia creeper. Watch for the vine around canyon streams and damp shadows.

Just after the trail makes two quick creek crossings, **bigtooth maple** trees ignite the scene.

At the Red Rock Pillars at mile 1.5, purple conglomerate bluffs squeeze into the canyon. The **bigtooth maple** trees like the moist environment the cliffs create. From here, the trail runs up and down the canyon walls, crisscrossing the stream. At Indian Creek Canyon, watch for trout in the pools that form where Indian and Lanphier Creeks merge.

After 0.5 mile, the trail starts to climb steeply up the canyon slope, leaving most of the color several hundred feet below. When the trail tops out, linger long enough to catch your breath and take in views

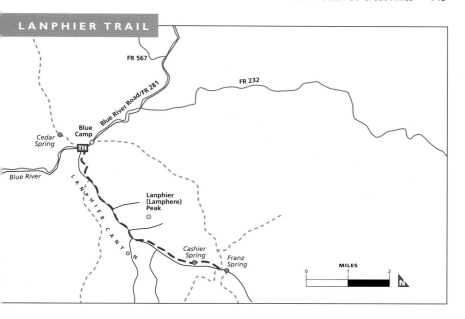

of Bear Mountain, Lanphier (Lamphere) Peak, and Lanphier Canyon. The trail then heads for the inner folds of the slopes. For the next mile, the trail rambles in and out of secluded basins filled with **Gambel oak**, then once again drops all the way into Lanphier Canyon and its colorful environment.

You may not notice the unassuming Whoa Canyon emptying into the creek on the right. According to one old timer in the area, the canyon's name was inspired by horse riders saying "whoa" to their mounts as they descended the steep canyon. You will, however, notice when the trail arrives at Cashier Spring at mile 5. The spring's lush environment attracts **bigtooth maple** trees.

D. Scott Marks, a rancher and early forest ranger who lived on the Blue River at the turn of the 20th century, inspired the name for the spring and the steep hill north of it (Banker's Hill). Marks compared gathering cattle off Banker's Hill and down to Cashier Spring with borrowing money from the bank. If successful, he said, it was like going to the cashier at the bank.

From Cashier Spring, it's 0.6 mile to the trail's end at its intersection with the Cow Flat Trail just northeast of Campbell Flat. A handful of **aspen** trees in a crook may surprise you as you start the climb out of the spring to Campbell Flat. The microclimate created at this low elevation allows the **aspen** to thrive. Unless you absolutely must finish the last segment of trail, which passes uneventfully through ponderosa pines up an intensely steep slope, let the anomalous **aspen** be your turnaround point.

Autumn Hike 38 # White House Trail

Beauty mixes with ancient history on this trail, which descends to the bottom of Canyon de Chelly. This is the only route in the canyon that you can access without a guide. The beauty begins at the trailhead, showing stunning views of the terra-cotta canyon walls that drip with desert varnish (dark pigments created from minerals, bacteria, and water) and swirl with crossbedding and erosion patterns. The walls stand perpendicular to the canyon floor, from which a continuous ribbon of **Fremont cottonwood** and **willow** trees emanates gold.

The historical aspect lies at the end of the trail at a ruin inhabited from A.D. 1040 to 1275. This 80-room ruin is one of the largest in the canyon.

The trail begins as a traipse across the slickrock rim, where you can see stunning views of the canyon and its fall color below. Sandstone rocks and rough-hewn steps demarcate the route. Once below the rim, the canyon's

TRAIL RATING	moderate
TRAIL LENGTH	1.25 miles one way
LOCATION	Chinle
ELEVATION	6,000–5,500 feet
CONTACT	Canyon de Chelly National Monument, 520-674-5500
PEAK COLOR	late October
SPECIAL CONSIDERATIONS	The Navajo request that you take no photos of personal property without prior permission.
DIRECTIONS	From US 191, go east 2 miles to Chinle. Turn east (right) onto Navajo 7 and drive 3 miles to Canyon de Chelly National Monument. Take South Rim Drive for 5.7 miles and turn north (left) onto the White House Ruin Overlook and Trailhead.

The White House Ruins in the Canyon de Chelly National Monument is a dramatic and enchanting destination within the surrounding Navajo lands.

enchanting atmosphere takes over. The walls change colors at the whim of the sun and shadows. Alcoves and windows carved into the canyon wall come into view. Juniper and piñon trees nestle in cracks and walk upon ledges.

Sumac bushes toss pretty shades of red onto the trail. The Navajo make baskets from the bushes by stripping the bark off the branches, then using the bark for twine as they form the branches into baskets.

TAMARISK
Tamarix pentandra

When the Department of Agriculture introduced tamarisk trees into the United States for erosion control at the turn of the 20th century, they had no idea of the trees' propensity to eventually overtake native plants in the lower elevations of the West. The trees prevailed where overgrazing and natural erosion weakened cottonwood and mesquite galleries. Today, the trend is toward eradicating the trees, and managing agencies and volunteer groups have made efforts to do this in the Grand Canyon.

Nevertheless, the trees do produce a striking fall color when their tiny, succulent leaves turn an orange-gold. If you do come across a tamarisk tree in the fall, its unique coloration will immediately capture your eyes.

As the trail continues in serpentine fashion down rippled sandstone, past shady alcoves and around undulating outcroppings, the scent from the piñon pines adds a lilt of sweetness to the air. Just before it hits the canyon floor, the trail burrows through a tunnel in the sandstone. At the end of the tunnel, when the trail passes a private residence, you'll catch a glimpse of how the Navajo live. With no electricity or running water, the Navajo continue their centuries-old lifestyle of farming and raising sheep.

Just past the residence, **willow** and **tamarisk** thickets, golden with fall color, canopy the trail as it heads for the canyon's sandy drainage. The trail crosses a footbridge and turns a bend, furnishing your first look at the ruins nestled in the sheer canyon wall less than 0.25 mile away. After you view the ruins and read about their history, return the way you came.

WHITE HOUSE TRAIL

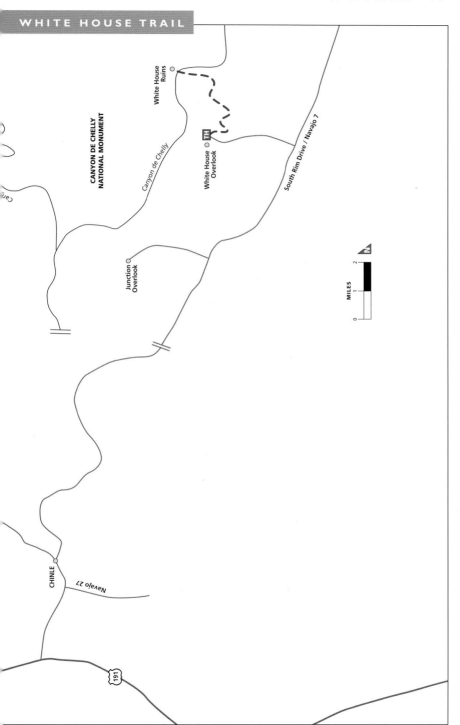

Autumn
Hike 39 # Aravaipa Canyon

Larry Ulrich

TRAIL RATING	moderate
TRAIL LENGTH	up to 11 miles one way
LOCATION	Superior
ELEVATION	2,630–3,060 feet
CONTACT	Bureau of Land Management, 520-348-4400
PEAK COLOR	mid-November

SPECIAL CONSIDERATIONS In this area, be sure to filter all creek water, beware of rattlesnakes in late fall and early spring, and watch for flash floods in wet weather.

Hikers must obtain a permit (with a three-day, two-night maximum stay) from the BLM Safford Field Office. You can make reservations up to 13 weeks in advance. Visitation is limited to 30 people per day on the west end, and the maximum group size is 10 people. A fee of $5 per person per day is payable at the trailhead.

DIRECTIONS From Superior on US 60, go south on Arizona 177 and drive 34 miles to Winkelman. Continue south on Arizona 77 and drive 11 miles to Aravaipa Road; turn left (east) and drive 12 miles to the parking area.

The Aravaipa Canyon Wilderness encompasses one of the most rugged and biologically diverse riparian environments in the state. You can expect a true wilderness experience on this hike as there are no established trails other than beaten paths that wind around undergrowth and weave back and forth across the creek. Sometimes wading the creek is the only route, so wear footgear you don't mind getting wet.

While you slosh through the creek's rushing waters, the sere desert and its prickly appointments linger just outside the creek's lush haven of a mixed broadleaf riparian plant community. The consistent ribbon of trees along the stream turns gold when **willow** thickets and **Arizona walnut**, **Arizona sycamore**, **velvet ash**, and **Fremont cottonwood** trees take on their fall color.

A few historical remnants lie along the creek, mostly at the east end of the canyon. According to historians and archaeologists, the Sobaipuri Indians cultivated farms that extended into the western end of the canyon. Apaches also spent time in the whole canyon, but left sparing clues.

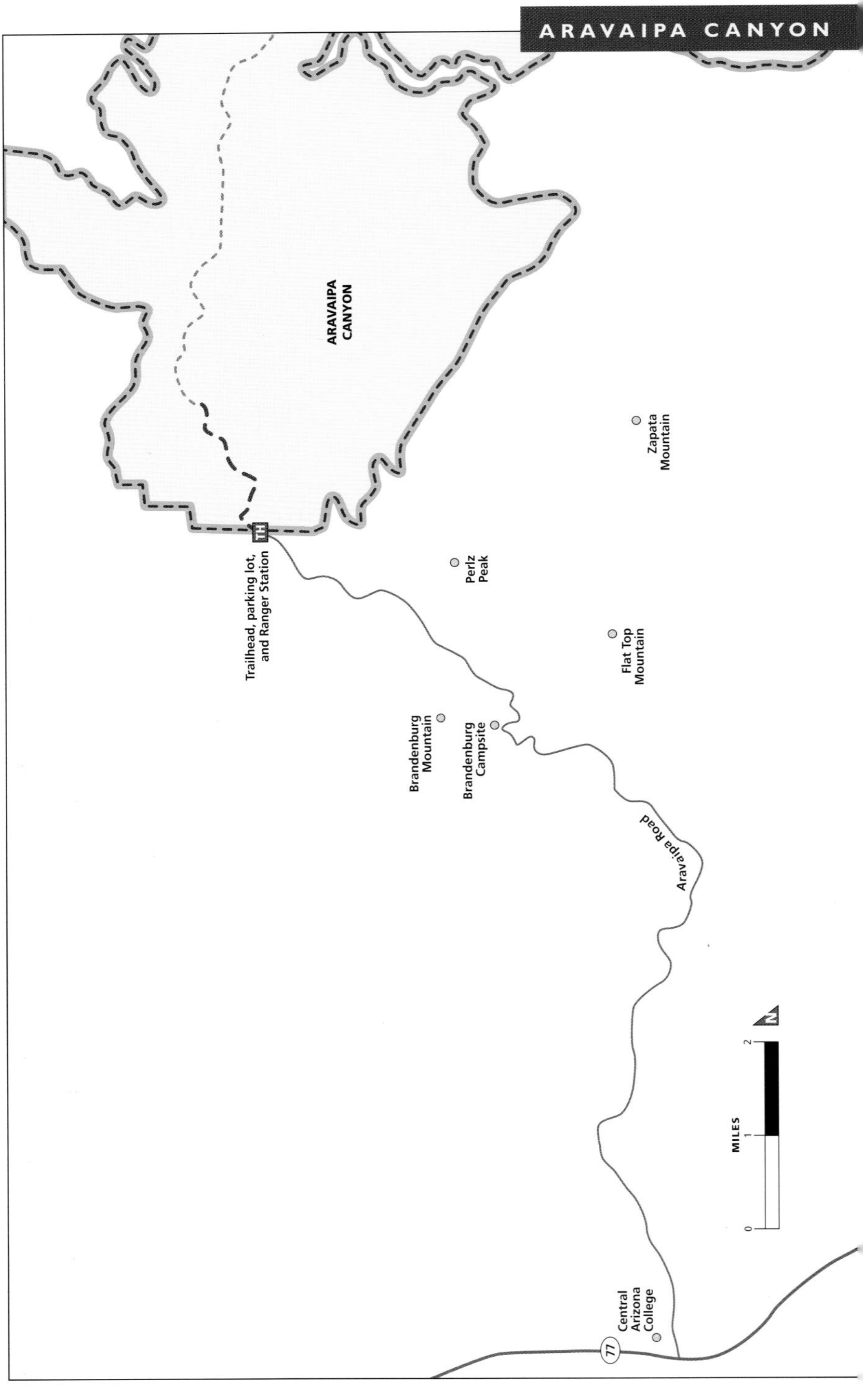

ARAVAIPA CANYON

ARAVAIPA
CANYON

Zapata
Mountain

Perlz
Peak

Flat Top
Mountain

Trailhead, parking lot,
and Ranger Station

Brandenburg
Mountain

Brandenburg
Campsite

Aravaipa Road

Central
Arizona
College

77

N

MILES

0   1   2

As the creek starts to squeeze between wine-red rhyolite cliffs around mile 2, imposing mountain peaks congregate around the narrowing canyon in an area nicknamed The Box. At mile 2.3, the narrows end. The canyon eventually widens enough to accommodate a beaten path that rambles through mesquite bosquets. You can explore several side canyons interspersed along the creek, some of which have pools that glow gold from reflections of **Fremont cottonwood** and **willow** trees.

Hiking is slow going in the canyon, and you should plan for a one-mile-per-hour hiking rate. The Box makes a good day-hike destination.

Aravaipa Creek's lush habitat presents a rich show of fall color for wading explorers in the canyon.

Autumn
Hike 40

Marshall Gulch–Aspen Trail

TRAIL RATING	moderate
TRAIL LENGTH	5.1 mile loop
LOCATION	Tucson
ELEVATION	7,410–8,400 feet
CONTACT	Coronado National Forest, 520-749-8700
PEAK COLOR	mid- to late October
SPECIAL CONSIDERATIONS	The Forest Service charges a $5 user fee per car.
DIRECTIONS	From I-10 in Tucson, drive east on Grant Road to Tanque Verde Road and continue east to the Catalina Highway. Turn left (north) and drive 25 miles up the mountain through the town of Summerhaven, and go south (left) on FR 10 about 1.5 miles to the trailhead.

This loop, one of the most popular hikes on Mt. Lemmon, passes through a diversified area. The route takes you from a lavish hardwood forest to a dry pine-oak forest, then back to a moisture-rich section of mixed conifers and **aspen** trees. Along the way, it stops to view the trademark granite formations and dramatic canyons of the Santa Catalina Mountains.

The environment the Marshall Gulch Trail enters, a streambed cocooned in a narrow gulch, nurtures moisture-loving plants and trees. **Bigtooth maple** trees, with their roots stretching across the trail like bony limbs, color the path with hues of yellow, orange, and red. Their leaves scatter on giant gray boulders shiny with mica or covered with moss. **Agrimonia**, a wildflower of the rose family, forms colonies around stream crossings that paint the ground with hues of yellow and red.

When the gulch narrows and the trail nudges up to a rockwall at about mile 0.6, **red-osier dogwood** and **willow** thickets fill the streambed with yellow and red colors. A few moments later, after climbing slightly above the stream, the trail passes another rockwall across the stream. Take a moment to peruse the wall, filled with pastel hues from a hanging garden of **coral bells**. The plant's round, scallop-edged leaves often color in the fall.

As the trail continues to climb, the **bigtooth maple** trees take a break. **Gambel oak** trees bring their golden color to the path until it levels off and enters another colony of **bigtooth maple** trees, this time joined by **velvet ash** trees. Look for a small stand of **aspen** trees at the trail's last creek crossing.

All the colors slowly evanesce as the trail parts company with the stream and climbs more seriously toward its end on Marshall Saddle. At the saddle, mile 1.3, take a hairpin left onto the Aspen Trail.

The Aspen Trail heads to the top of a ridge as it continues its climb through an evergreen belt of pines, firs, and oaks on the western side of Marshall Peak. The first signs of color come at about mile 2.1, where you'll see flecks of gold from **New Mexico locust** bushes. **Gambel oak** trees appear at about mile 2.7, lined up along both sides of the trail.

When the trail crests the ridge and turns away from the western exposure into a cooler and moister environment, you begin to see occasional **bigtooth maple** and **boxelder** trees. As the trail starts to switchback down the mountain, stands of **aspen** appear.

During the last 0.5 mile, the bold walls of Sabino Canyon —one of the trail's main attractions—rise on the right. The trail ends back at the Marshall Gulch parking area.

RED-OSIER DOGWOOD
Cornus stolonifera

Favoring moisture-rich niches in canyons or banks along waterways, the red-osier dogwood bush makes a stunning addition to a trail's spread of fall color. The leaves turn yellow, rose, or maroon colors, and even when they've fallen, the trees' wine-colored stems make an attractive sight.

The labyrinth of roots in colonies of red-osier dogwood create effective erosion controls. The bush spreads by supine stems taking root.

Named for the color of its stems (red) and the supple willow branches it mimics (osier), the bark of the red-osier dogwood is used for basketry and twine. Its leaves were often an addition to kinnikinnick, a tobacco substitute smoked by pioneers and American Indians.

MARSHALL GULCH–ASPEN TRAIL

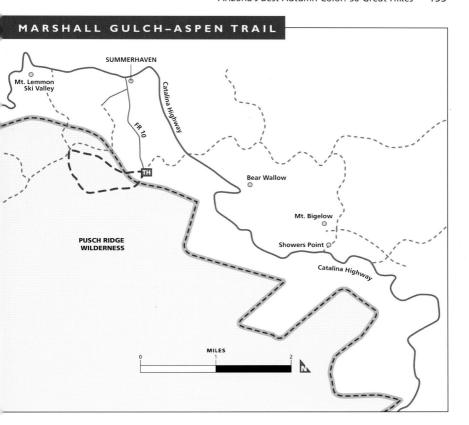

SUMMERHAVEN

Mt. Lemmon
Ski Valley

Catalina Highway

FR 10

TH

Bear Wallow

Mt. Bigelow

PUSCH RIDGE
WILDERNESS

Showers Point

Catalina Highway

MILES

0   1   2

N

Autumn
Hike 41

Butterfly Trail

Larry Ulrich

TRAIL RATING	strenuous
TRAIL LENGTH	5.2 miles one way
LOCATION	Tucson
ELEVATION	8,400–6,700 feet
CONTACT	Coronado National Forest, 520-749-8700
PEAK COLOR	mid-October
SPECIAL CONSIDERATIONS	The Forest Service charges a $5 user fee per car at this trailhead. This hike makes a good shuttle. The other trailhead is located at Mt. Bigelow (from the Catalina Highway, turn right onto the road to Mt. Bigelow, go 0.1 mile and turn right toward Mt. Bigelow, and then drive 1.2 miles to the trailhead).
DIRECTIONS	From I-10 in Tucson, drive east on Grant Road to Tanque Verde Road and continue east to the Catalina Highway. Turn left (north) and drive past milepost 23 to the trailhead.

Trail designer Fred Kimball, who commented on the proliferation of butterflies in the area, probably named the Butterfly Trail. The trail takes you through many different biomes and microclimates that produce dramatic displays of fall color. Prompted by the great diversity of vegetation in the area, Kimball also initiated the 1,000-acre Butterfly Research Natural Area that the trail passes through. Nearby Butterfly Peak gets its name from the natural area.

The trail starts out showing off views of Alder Canyon in the east as it drops into a mixed conifer forest and switchbacks steeply toward Novio Spring. Within the first 0.5 mile, **bigtooth maple** trees appear in the moist crooks of the mountainside, then disappear to let **Gambel oak** provide the color. Views of the copper smelter at the San Manuel Mine simmer along the eastern horizon.

At mile 1.4, you'll come to the intersection with the Crystal Spring Trail. About 100 yards uphill from a primitive camp lies the wreckage of one of two fighter jets that collided over the area during the 1950s. One jet crashed along the Mt. Lemmon Highway (the road from Summerhaven to Oracle, also called the Control Road); the other crashed near Crystal Spring. The pilots managed to parachute to safety.

Continue on the Butterfly Trail as it drops down toward Novio Spring ("novio" means "boyfriend" in Spanish). For the next mile, the trail alternates between oak communities and the cover of mixed conifers. **Boxelder** and **bigtooth maple** trees gather among the conifers in moist ravines. Watch for

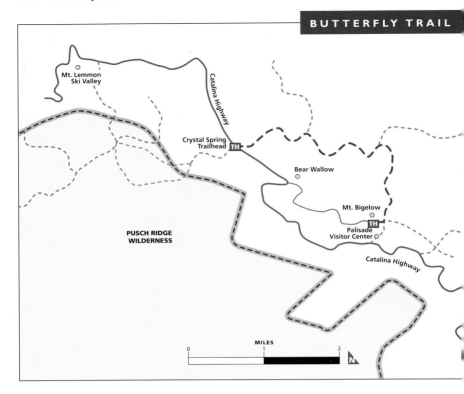

errant stands of **aspen** trying to hold their ground among the conifers, which have a propensity to squeeze them out

As the trail nears Novio Spring, fall colors start to dominate with brilliant displays of red and gold. **Poison ivy** cloaks the ground in crimson. Once at the Novio Spring, the drainage becomes a collage of color, with the gold of **Arizona walnut** and **velvet ash** trees, and touches of red tones from **bigtooth maple** trees. **Virginia creeper** adds trails of scarlet as it crawls along the path.

The fall color follows as the trail climbs out of the drainage, then dwindles to russet and gold from **Gambel oak** trees around the intersection with the Davis Spring Trail. Continue climbing on the Butterfly Trail.

When the trail passes through mixed conifers, **bigtooth maple** trees make temperamental appearances with **boxelder** in moist crooks. An **aspen** stand buried in the conifers supplies a burst of gold. By the last mile, the color returns more regularly, then evanesces slowly as the trail climbs through a shadowy fir forest.

At another intersection, follow the trail that leads 0.2 mile to Mt. Bigelow, then return the way you came if you have not set up a shuttle.

Sycamore Reservoir Trail

TRAIL RATING	strenuous
TRAIL LENGTH	2 miles one way
LOCATION	Tucson
ELEVATION	5,000–4,500 feet
CONTACT	Coronado National Forest, 520-749-8700
PEAK COLOR	mid-November
DIRECTIONS	From I-10 in Tucson, drive east on Grant Road to Tanque Verde Road and continue east to the Catalina Highway. Turn left onto the Catalina Highway and drive north up the mountain to just past milepost 7. Turn left onto the Old Prison Camp road and drive 0.5 mile to the trailhead.

Once a road that traveled from an old federal prison (a minimum security work camp) down to a reservoir at Sycamore Creek, this trail takes you to a pocket of golden foliage tucked away at the confluence of Bear and Sycamore Canyons. This route is also part of the Arizona Trail, the 790-mile route that travels between Arizona's northern and southern borders.

The first mile of the hike starts on the Molino Basin Trail where the prison once stood. In the late 1940s to early 1950s, the prisoners (mostly illegal Mexican immigrants) built the Catalina Highway that runs up the mountain. They also built campgrounds and side roads on the mountain.

The reservoir the trail leads to supplied water to the prison. Remnants of the pipe the water pumped through remain along sections of the trail.

At mile 0.2, the trail crosses a streambed where a handful of **Fremont cottonwood** trees take advantage of the intermittent flow of water during wet weather. For the next 0.75 mile, as the trail climbs up the east face of Gibbon Mountain, the vegetation sticks to oaks and junipers spreading over rounded hillsides. When the trail tops out at an old parking area at mile 1, the scene switches from rounded slopes to a fabulous panorama of the craggy ridgeline of Mt. Lemmon.

The Sycamore Reservoir Trail starts where a large metal sign announces the Arizona Trail. The path switchbacks about 800 feet in 1 mile down the north face of Gibbon Mountain to the reservoir. Flash floods have silted the reservoir, but the concrete wall remains where water from Sycamore Creek cascades down a spillway into Bear Canyon.

SYCAMORE RESERVOIR TRAIL

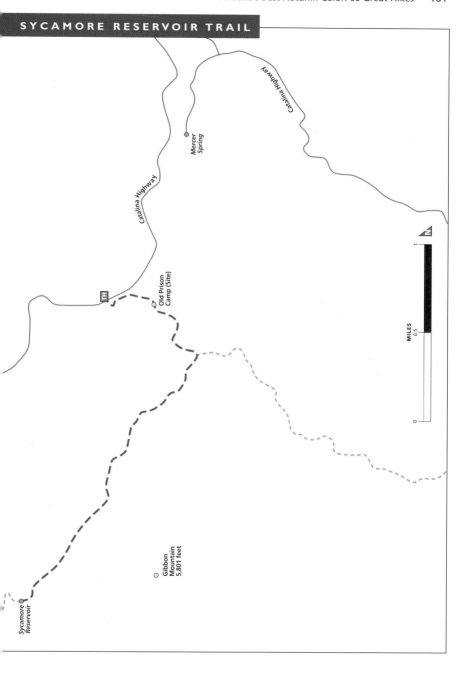

Catalina Highway

Mercer
Spring

Catalina Highway

Old Prison
Camp (Site)

TH

Gibbon
Mountain
5,801 feet

Sycamore
Reservoir

MILES

0   0.5   1

The reservoir is now filled with a collection of **Fremont cottonwood, Arizona sycamore,** and **willow** trees which color gold in the fall. If you continue heading north up the gravel-bottomed streambed of Sycamore Canyon, the trees follow. In about 0.25 mile, a bench that provides some nice campsites narrows the bed, forcing you to rock hop if you continue. Return the way that you came.

FREMONT COTTONWOOD
Populus fremontii

Fremont cottonwood trees can reach gigantic sizes. The largest one in Arizona, located on Sonoita Creek near Patagonia, measures 42 feet in circumference (approximately 13.5 feet in diameter), 92 feet high, and 108 feet at its crown. According to tree expert Ken Morrow of the *Arizona Register of Big Trees* (the Arizona chapter of the *National Register of Big Trees*), the tree is also the biggest living tree of any species in Arizona. Most cottonwoods, however, average about 50 feet tall with a 3-foot diameter.

In the springtime, the fluffy seeds covered with white cotton gather like clouds of snow on the landscape. The finely-toothed leaves turn a lovely gold in the fall.

Hopi Indians use the roots of Fremont cottonwood trees for Kachina dolls and drums. Navajo artists prefer this wood for their whimsical folk art. Beavers favor the wood for food and dams.

Bluff Loop

TRAIL RATING	easy
TRAIL LENGTH	3.1 mile loop
LOCATION	Tucson
ELEVATION	2,800–3,000 feet
CONTACT	Coronado National Forest, 520-749-8700
PEAK COLOR	mid-November
SPECIAL CONSIDERATIONS	Sabino Canyon Road is closed to all motorized vehicles inside the Sabino Canyon Recreation Area (except the concession trams). Tram rides are available for $5 per person. For this hike, you may take a tram to stop #1, hike the Lake Trail to the Bluff Trail, and continue as described below. The recreation area charges a $5 parking fee.
DIRECTIONS	From I-10 at Kino, drive east on Orange Grove Road to Sunrise Drive. Continue east on Sunrise Drive, then veer north (left) onto Sabino Canyon Road to the trailhead.

During the first 0.7 mile of the hike as the route follows Sabino Canyon Road from the parking area to the trailhead, the Upper Sonoran vegetation of Sabino Canyon never gives a clue of the beautiful spread of colors on the Bluff Trail. Saguaro cacti, palo verde trees, and cholla and prickly pear cacti cover the surrounding slopes. You can hike the roadway or the path that parallels it for most of the way.

At a ridge top, the path ends and forces you onto the roadway. At this point, you'll see glimpses of the fall color gathered along Sabino Creek. Watch for trams and bicycles as you hike 0.1 mile to the Bluff Trailhead on the east side of the roadway.

The Bluff Trail makes a quick drop into the Sabino Creek drainage, right in the heart of the canyon's fall color. **Velvet ash**, **cottonwood**, and **willow** trees create an intense glow of gold and **Arizona sycamore** trees add honey brown. A forest of saguaro cacti watches from the canyon walls.

At mile 0.9, you'll come to a scattering of picnic benches and grills at the edge of a bench overlooking the streambed. If you're lucky, you might see some coatimundi passing through, looking like so many monkeys with their proud tails standing in the air.

In another 0.1 mile, the trail passes the Sabino Dam. The Civilian Conservation Corps, a work relief program set up by the federal government during the Depression in the 1930s, built the dam as well as the bridges crossing

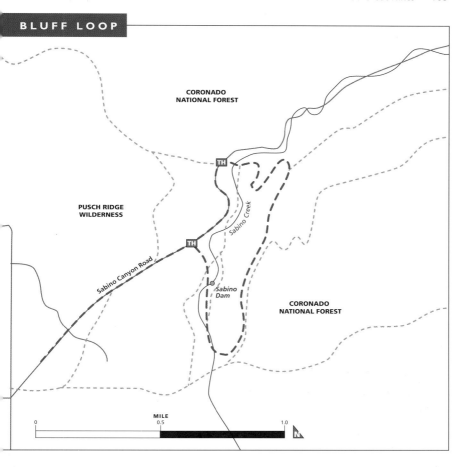

BLUFF LOOP

the creek. Before the lake filled up with leaf mold and silt, the government stocked the lake with trout, making it a popular fishing spot for about 10 years. After one dredging, the lake filled up again, and it has never been dredged since.

Continue on the path another 0.1 mile to the Dam Bridge. Cross the bridge, then turn left onto the Dam Trail. At mile 1.3, you come to the junction with the Lake Trail. Continue straight on the Lake Trail.

The Lake Trail enters a secluded corridor along Sabino Creek between the creek's golden riparian cover and the Upper Sonoran vegetation running up the surrounding mountain slopes. The dense growth cloisters the path with a remote atmosphere. At the junction with the Phoneline Trail at about mile 1.8, continue on the Lake Trail. In about 100 feet, the trail approaches the creek bed, picking through a rocky bank, then rock hops across the creek back to Sabino Canyon Road. Turn left onto the roadway and follow it 1.2 miles back to the parking area.

Autumn
Hike 44 # Ash Creek Trail

Larry Ulrich

In its entirety, the Ash Creek Trail travels an 8.2-mile downhill course to the desert floor. However, the best display of fall color appears in its upper reaches, above Ash Creek Falls. Though you won't be traveling far, keep in mind that the hike back to the trailhead is a strenuous uphill trek.

The trail starts in a corridor of young **aspen** trees that glow gold and Douglas firs that saturate the air with a sugary pine smell. Just beyond the ruins of an old log shack (probably built and used back when a sawmill ran near Ash Creek Falls), you'll catch **Rocky Mountain maple** trees making a spotty appearance. Though not as colorful as the **bigtooth maple** trees that appear at lower elevations, the **Rocky Mountain maple** trees add hues of red to the landscape. As the trail zigzags downward to Ash Creek, more mature **aspen** trees mingle with the firs, adding a golden shimmer to the dark green

TRAIL RATING	difficult
TRAIL LENGTH	2.5–8.2 miles one way
LOCATION	Mount Graham
ELEVATION	9,490–8,200 feet
CONTACT	Coronado National Forest, 520-428-4150
PEAK COLOR	early October
DIRECTIONS	From Safford, take US 191 south about 7 miles to Arizona 366. Turn southwest (right) and drive 29 miles to the trailhead.

forest. Once you are creekside, **Rocky Mountain maple** trees converge on the trail.

The reddish color continues when the trail hits a high spot above the creek just after the intersection with the Webb Peak Trail. A rusty piece of machinery stands right by the trail signs, a remnant from the mountain's logging days. Several sawmills once operated across the whole mountain. The pieces of machinery along the Ash Creek Trail come from the mill once located on a flat at Ash Creek Falls in the 1930s. The falls served as a flume for the mill.

Most of the color evanesces when the trail enters a meadow that puts a wedge between it and Ash Creek. After a short distance, the canyon begins to narrow and pushes the creek closer to the trail. When the trail practically rubs shoulders with the creek, **red-osier dogwood** bushes make a showy display of gold and reds. Look for **Rocky Mountain maple** trees standing streamside across the creek.

At about 1.7 miles, the trail comes to an ancillary path constructed for horses to detour an upcoming section of slickrock. To stay on the main trail, veer right. The trail squeezes between the creek and slickrock outcroppings as it barges through a thicket of **red-osier dogwood** before reaching a dicey creek crossing.

After a short sprint up the canyon wall, the trail takes on the feel of a ledgelike path as it overlooks the creek. If you look down into the creek, you'll notice a strapping stand of **aspen** trees. When the trail makes a final creek crossing at a slab of slickrock down which Ash Creek Falls slithers, watch for

Gambel oak trees adding hues of gold and russet to the mix of gold and red from the **aspen** and **Rocky Mountain maple** trees encroaching the trail.

Just after the horse detour comes back to the trail, a rocky viewpoint allows rugged, but exquisite, views of the canyon and 200-foot Ash Creek Falls. Return the way you came.

BIGTOOTH MAPLE
Acer grandidentatum

Much of the lively fall colors in Arizona come from bigtooth maple trees, with leaves that turn hues of yellow, orange, and red. The trees go by another name as well, canyon maple, because their favorite environment lies in canyons at 4,000- to 8,000-foot elevations. Sometimes tapped for maple sugar, the bigtooth maple is the Southwest's answer to the sugar maple.

Much more colorful than Rocky Mountain maple, *(Acer glabrum)*these trees also differ in leaf and trunk features. The leaves of both trees have three lobes, but the bigtooths' leaves have big teeth and their light brown trunks have shallow furrows. The Rocky Mountain maple leaves, in contrast, have fine teeth and their smooth gray trunks are often many stemmed. Rocky Mountain maples generally appear in higher elevations, and they produce a nice show of yellow to reddish leaves in the fall.

ASH CREEK TRAIL

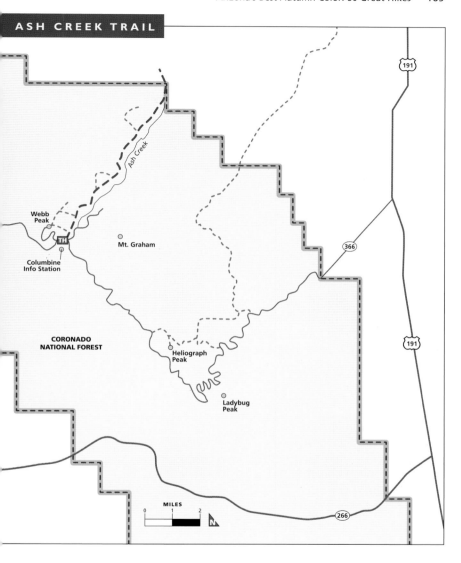

Ash Creek

Webb
Peak

TH

Mt. Graham

Columbine
Info Station

191

366

191

CORONADO
NATIONAL FOREST

Heliograph
Peak

Ladybug
Peak

MILES

0   1   2

N

266

Autumn
Hike 45   *Arcadia and*
Heliograph Trails

TRAIL RATING	strenuous
TRAIL LENGTH	5.1–6.1 miles one way
LOCATION	Safford
ELEVATION	6,700–10,022 feet
CONTACT	Coronado National Forest, 520-428-4150
PEAK COLOR	early October
DIRECTIONS	From Safford, take US 191 south about 7 miles to Arizona 366. Turn southwest (right) and drive 10.8 miles to the trailhead in the Upper Arcadia Campground.

Starting at the end of the Upper Arcadia Campground, the Arcadia Trail begins its 4-mile, 2,700-foot climb up to its junction with the Heliograph Trail in a ponderosa pine forest. As the trail climbs, it passes moist crevices in Wet Canyon filled with the yellows of **boxelder** and **aspen** trees or red hues of **bigtooth maple** trees. Sometimes, the path glances at distant views of southeast Arizona.

In its second mile, the trail plods through a ponderosa pine forest. Watch for **creeping barberry** to blush red along the trail and seek out the occasional outcroppings that jut through the forest to allow panoramic views. You might see the Peloncillo Mountains rubbing against the New Mexico border in the east or the Cabezas Mountains running into the Chiricahua Mountains in the southeast.

By mile 3, **aspen** trees make a regular appearance and extraordinarily tall Douglas fir and Engelmann spruce trees, shaggy with moss, perfume the air. Bold gray outcroppings push their way through yellowed thickets of **New Mexico locust** trees that infringe upon the trail, and more views appear. Because of the trail's exceptional views, it has been designated as a National Recreation Trail, distinguishing it with the best trails in the nation.

At the trail's intersection with the Heliograph Trail, you can continue on the Arcadia Trail another mile as it descends to its end at the Shannon Campground. Or, you can take a side hike up the 1 mile-long trail that climbs to Heliograph Peak. Named for the signal mirrors, called heliographs, used during an 1880 campaign against Geronimo and his Apache warriors, the peak is now a lookout tower that signals fires from May 1 through July 31.

The Heliograph Trail's 800-foot ascent takes you through beaming **aspen** stands. On the peak, the trail features fabulous vistas in almost every direction. When you have returned to the Arcadia Trail, continue 1.1 miles to the Shannon Campground on the Arcadia Trail or return the way you came.

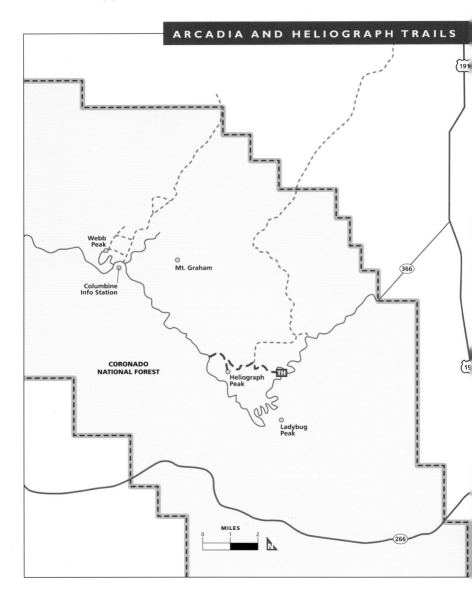

ARCADIA AND HELIOGRAPH TRAILS

San Pedro Trail

TRAIL RATING	easy to difficult
TRAIL LENGTH	1–11 miles one way
LOCATION	Sierra Vista
ELEVATION	4,000–4,200 feet
CONTACT	Bureau of Land Management, 520-458-3559
PEAK COLOR	mid-November
DIRECTIONS	From the intersection of Arizona 92 and 90 in Sierra Vista, drive east on Arizona 90 about 6.4 miles to the turnoff for the San Pedro House and turn right (south). Drive 0.2 mile to the trailhead.

The San Pedro Trail, a work in progress that may eventually span 40 miles from the Mexican border to the town of St. David, travels through much of the San Pedro Riparian National Conservation Area. The area draws an impressive show of seasonal birds. A total of 360 species of birds have been recorded in the San Pedro habitat, making it one of the best bird-watching sites in the nation. If you intend to hike all the way to Hereford, a shuttle is necessary, as it will take you at least eight hours. Start early and wear footgear you don't mind getting wet.

The hike starts just east of the San Pedro House, crossing a field where hawks often glide as they peruse the ground for food. In 0.25 mile, you'll come to a bench near the San Pedro riverbed. The thick line of **Goodding willow** and **Fremont cottonwood** trees forms a golden wall that twists and turns with the river. Follow the trail as it turns right at a sitting bench and heads 0.1 mile to another sitting bench. At this point, you may continue on the nature trail or veer left on a beaten path dropping into the riverbed. For the hike described here, veer left.

The path heads south along the river under the cover of **Goodding willow** and **Fremont cottonwood** trees. **Cottonwood/willow** forests supply the most productive wildlife habitats in the nation. You'll see **velvet ash** trees along the riverbanks as well.

In about 0.5 mile, the trail turns right, edging the Green Kingfisher Pond, and then makes a loop back through the meadow to the San Pedro House. But you may continue on the beaten path. If you do, you'll start to notice animal prints in the silty soil—deer hooves, bobcat paws, and raccoon feet. The path fades out by about mile 1.3.

The San Pedro National Conservation Area protects wildlife, luxurious vegetation, and, most famously, a great variety of aquatic birds that visit the San Pedro River.

If you continue the hike southward, you'll experience a fascinating adventure. **Fremont cottonwood** leaves sprinkle like gold glitter in the sunshine and add to the carpet of leaves already laid on the forest floor. The flood-racked landscape starts to take on a primitive look and exudes a wild atmosphere. You may catch glimpses of owls flapping just below the treetops. The snap of a twig might flush a skittish giant blue heron from the water.

The midsection of the hike will require bushwhacking and wading the river. The last 2 miles before Hereford Road follow a beaten path.

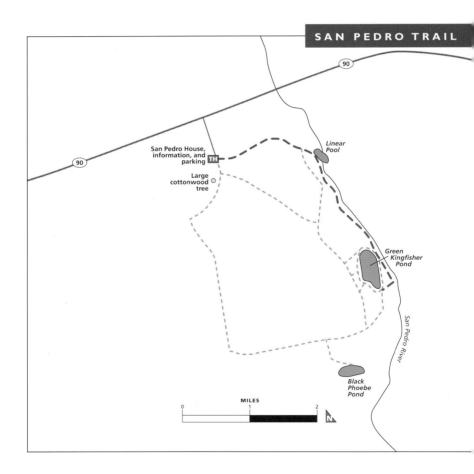

Ramsey Canyon Trail

TRAIL RATING	moderate
TRAIL LENGTH	0.7–3.5 miles one way
LOCATION	Sierra Vista
ELEVATION	5,700–8,075 feet
CONTACT	Ramsey Canyon Preserve, 520-378-2785
PEAK COLOR	mid- to late October
SPECIAL CONSIDERATIONS	The Nature Conservancy charges a $5 user fee per person.
DIRECTIONS	Drive 6 miles south of Sierra Vista on Arizona 92 to Ramsey Canyon Road. Turn west (right) and follow Ramsey Canyon Road 3.5 miles to the Nature Conservancy's Ramsey Canyon Preserve parking area and trailhead.

Situated in the Nature Conservancy's Mile Hi/Ramsey Canyon Preserve on the east face of the Huachuca Mountains, the trail begins its colorful route right in the preserve's information center. On the way out the back door, where the path actually begins, you can learn about the canyon and its wildlife from the informative displays in the center.

The Ramsey Canyon Preserve has developed a worldwide reputation for its large variety of hummingbirds. During the fall, you may see several of its 41 resident birds or any of up to two dozen migrants, which vary weekly.

Out on the beginning of the trail, where Ramsey Creek pours over boulders and slushes around rocks, **Arizona sycamore** trees gather around the rollicking waters. As soon as the trail climbs out of the drainage and onto an old road to follow a sign pointing toward the Hamburg Trail, the rest of the color shows up. **Bigtooth maple** and **velvet ash** trees, mixed in with evergreen Emory oak trees, gather around the road tossing their yellow and red leaves. **Fremont cottonwood** and **willow** trees glow golden along the creek banks.

Within 0.25 mile, you can see an old cabin across the stream from a viewpoint next to a peach tree with leaves that darken in autumn to a maroon color. Historic apple trees, left over from the homesteaders, also punctuate the area with a blush to their leaves.

You might catch deer browsing nonchalantly in the tall grasses on the side of the road. Protected on the conservancy property, the deer have an insouciant attitude toward hikers, which allows for good picture taking.

RAMSEY CANYON TRAIL

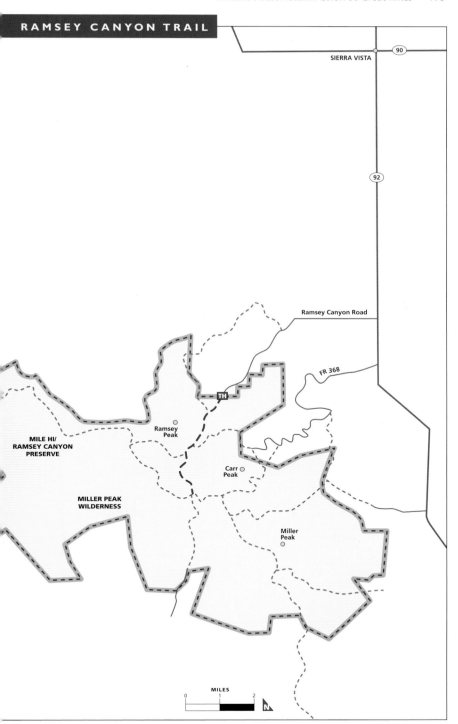

SIERRA VISTA

90

92

Ramsey Canyon Road

FR 368

TH

MILE HI/
RAMSEY CANYON
PRESERVE

Ramsey
Peak

Carr
Peak

MILLER PEAK
WILDERNESS

Miller
Peak

MILES

0   1   2

The trail starts to climb near a homestead at about mile 0.5. A bit farther, **bigtooth maple** and **Arizona sycamore** trees reflect their colors in the Frog Conservation Pond—the only place in the world where the Ramsey Canyon leopard frog lives. By the time the leaves change colors, the frogs will be hibernating in the mud and leaf litter at the bottom of the Frog Pond.

Just past the pond near a sprawling **Arizona sycamore** tree, Fletcher's Dance Hall once entertained the visitors who came to the canyon. The dance hall, which is no longer standing, featured German musicians.

From the Frog Pond, you may continue the hike on the single-track Hamburg Trail veering to the left. At mile 0.7, the trail crosses the boundary into the Coronado National Forest and then into the Miller Peak Wilderness area. The path cuts through an evergreen forest of mixed oaks for about 1 mile up to a ridge called the Ramsey Overlook. At the overlook, you can look down on the multicolored braid of fall foliage following the creek and a line of gold from **Goodding willow** and **Fremont cottonwood** trees along the San Pedro River to the east.

The trail drops into the canyon's drainage and crosses the creek, then starts climbing the canyon again. At mile 2.2, the trail arrives at the intersection with the Brown Trail. Continue straight on the Hamburg Trail.

During the next mile, the trail passes through a particularly lush environment where **bigtooth maple, Gambel oak**, and **Arizona sycamore** trees color its route as it wavers back and forth across the creek bed. At mile 3, the Carr Canyon Trail veers to the left. Continue straight as the trail enters Hamburg Meadow. During the mountain's mining days in the early 20th century, the miners working in surrounding mine tunnels stayed in Hamburg Meadow. Take a moment to view Ramsey Peak in the white cliffs to the north. The cliffs may have been created when an earthquake in 1887 crumbled half the peak into the canyon.

Just past the edge of Hamburg Meadow, the trail junctions with the Pat Scott Canyon Trail. The Hamburg Trail continues up Wisconsin Canyon until it ends at the Crest Trail at Bear Saddle. Return the way you came.

Scheelite Canyon Trail

Larry Ulrich

TRAIL RATING	moderate (first half) and strenuous (second half)
TRAIL LENGTH	4 miles one way
LOCATION	Fort Huachuca in Sierra Vista
ELEVATION	5,525–8,350 feet
CONTACT	Coronado National Forest, 520-378-0311
PEAK COLOR	end of October to early November
SPECIAL CONSIDERATIONS	Mechanized vehicles, including mountain bikes, are not allowed on this trail.
DIRECTIONS	From Sierra Vista, enter the main gate of Fort Huachuca. Stay on the main road for 9.5 miles, following the signs to Garden Canyon at all intersections. The trailhead starts 0.7 mile from where the pavement ends.

Hiking the Scheelite Canyon Trail can turn into an exciting experience if you have a chance meeting with the wildlife that frequent the steep gorge. You may catch sight of a colony of female coatimundi scampering up trees or a solo male traipsing across a tree branch. In this remote location, you might see a black bear clamoring down a pine tree with her youngster following. Mexican spotted owls, protected by the Endangered Species Act, frequent the canyon, and elegant trogons make rare appearances. If you do spot any wildlife, watch with respect and caution.

Cocooned in a wooded canyon, the trail starts its almost nonstop climb along a drainage that eventually ends on Scheelite Ridge. The moist environment nurtures continuous stands of **Gambel oak**, **bigtooth maple**, and **velvet ash** trees, creating one of the best displays of fall color in southeastern Arizona.

The **bigtooth maple** trees appear in the first 0.5 mile of the trail. They lean into the canyon's squat walls and reach into the trail as it climbs and crisscrosses the drainage. **Canyon grape** coils around rocks and trees, adding hues of gold.

Almost 1 mile into the trail, the canyon walls grow and the trail brushes past a smooth perpendicular wall to the right of the drainage. The **bigtooth maple** trees stretch their limbs to reach the sunlight, forming a rosy ceiling over the drainage. On the opposite side of the drainage, the trail passes a huge honeycombed limestone boulder as gnarly as the **Gambel oak** trees that surround it. The canyon's steel gray walls and the old logs strewn in the drainage give the canyon an untamed feel.

The trail crosses a section of bedrock, then bends to the left where **velvet ash** trees appear and light the canyon with their golden color. The trail takes a rocky route up the canyon wall and peers down upon the color. After the trail climbs a stretch of rocky stair steps and squeezes between boulders, the canyon floor meets up with the trail again.

For the next 0.25 mile, the trail settles down to a near level course. Then it's up and climbing again to the top of the west wall where it waits for the drainage to catch up so it can make another stream crossing.

Soon, the canyon narrows enough to force the trail into a drainage where **poison ivy** adds a scarlet blanket. Be careful negotiating this segment, as any brush with the three-leaved **poison ivy** plant can cause a toxic effect.

The trail continues in the drainage for a while, clamoring over dryfalls under a scarlet canopy of **bigtooth maples**. As the canyon opens up momentarily, the trail walks over a slab of bedrock through which a stream has cut a trough, then drops back into the drainage when the canyon closes up again. After another section of bedrock, watch for cairns on the left that lead you around a dryfall.

Finally, the canyon widens enough for the trail to separate from the drainage and start a painless uphill climb for about 0.5 mile. Then, the path resumes its steep ascent, climbing up the canyon walls where **Gambel oak** trees hang on until the

VELVET ASH
Fraxinus velutina

Most of the ash trees found in Arizona are velvet ash. The velvet on their young leaves—which inspires the tree's name—differentiates velvet ash from other ash trees and wears off as they mature. Found in canyon bottoms and wet washes, the trees illuminate the area with their bright gold fall color.

drainage meets up with the trail. Here, the golds and reds of moisture-loving **bigtooth maple** and **velvet ash** trees abound, and streamers of **Virginia creeper** trail from trees and crawl over rocks along the drainage.

The trail repeats this process, then finally leaves the **bigtooth maple** trees behind at mile 2.5, where it starts a relentlessly steep slog up to the Crest Trail. The **velvet ash** trees stop growing just before the last mile, but the **Gambel oak** trees follow you up to the rim. Watch for vibrant stands of **aspen** shining gold in the midst of the **oaks'** russet.

Once on the ridge, you are privy to incredible views of the surrounding mountainsides and the city of Sierra Vista. Return the way you came.

Rocky stairs assist the hardy hiker in a typically steep and rugged stretch of the Scheelite Canyon Trail.

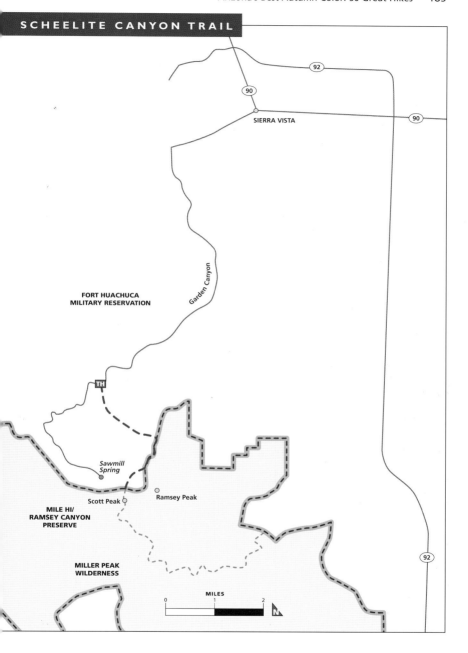

SCHEELITE CANYON TRAIL

Miller Canyon Trail

TRAIL RATING	strenuous
TRAIL LENGTH	4 miles one way
LOCATION	Sierra Vista
ELEVATION	5,750–8,550 feet
CONTACT	Coronado National Forest, 520-378-0311
PEAK COLOR	early November
SPECIAL CONSIDERATIONS	Most of the Miller Canyon Trail is located in the Miller Peak Wilderness, where no mechanized vehicles, including mountain bikes, are allowed.
DIRECTIONS	From the intersection of Arizona 92 and 90 in Sierra Vista, drive south on Arizona 92 for 8.4 miles to Miller Canyon Road (FR 56) and turn west (right). Drive 2.4 miles to the trailhead.

Before 1927, Miller Canyon was called Mill Canyon. The name change memorialized John Miller, who raised produce in the canyon.

The Miller Canyon Trail sets an uphill pace from its beginning as it switchbacks through an evergreen forest of piñon pines, manzanita bushes, juniper trees, and a variety of oaks. But by the time you reach the Miller Peak Wilderness at about mile 0.5, you get a hint of the rich fall display waiting farther up the trail.

Just beyond the fruit orchard at Beatty's Miller Canyon Guest Ranch and Orchard along the Miller Canyon drainage below, you'll see a line of **Arizona sycamore** and **Fremont cottonwood** trees coloring the landscape tan and yellow. **Skunkbushes**, with their puzzle-piece arrangement of leaf colors ranging from yellow to salmon to drop-dead red, start to brighten the path as they cozy up to the trail. **Bigtooth maple** trees make a brief visit at a drainage crossing, but generally stay hidden behind the evergreen forest between the trail (an old road at this point) and the canyon drainage. Some color, mostly from **velvet ash** and a few **bigtooth maple** trees, ventures out to the trail.

At about mile 0.6, the trail approaches the Hunter Canyon trail junction and, just beyond it, a fork in the road. If you veer left at the fork, you can visit an old sawmill site situated about 0.1 mile away along Miller Creek. To continue on the trail, veer right. In about 0.25 mile, the road picks through Miller Creek and crosses over to the south side of the canyon to start the most colorful segment of the hike.

By mile 1, the path climbs above the creek into a pine forest. For the next mile, the trail parallels the stream and reveals a striking display of color emanating from **bigtooth maple** trees on the banks below. **Velvet ash** trees crowd next to the trail and add a gold glow to the pines' shadows.

Though probably the most beautiful—and certainly the most colorful—section of the trail, this section has a demanding personality as it climbs with the canyon up the side of the mountain. Along the way, watch for an adit gaping on the left with a sign instructing you to stay out. Old mines may have unstable walls and structures inside, as well as sudden pits, so stick to the trail.

At mile 2, the trail crosses the drainage to the north side and leaves much of the color behind. This makes a good turnaround point for a short day hike, or you can continue to the trail's end at the Crest Trail.

The trail starts to switchback up the canyon in an evergreen environment of pine, fir, and oak trees. A stream crossing at mile 2.5 attracts a group of **Gambel oak** trees that add gold and russet hues. At mile 3, watch for a rusted old steam boiler dragged up the canyon by prospector Max Baumkirchner to process his ore. Right behind the clunky machinery, you'll see a stand of **aspen**.

The trail resumes its steady climb up the canyon and enters an exposed burn area. Without the cover of trees, you can see the mountains' craggy rock faces surrounding the trail and a panorama of the Chiricahua Mountains to the east. **Gambel oak** trees follow the trail, making spotty appearances as the path switches back and forth in the canyon. Just before it ends, Bathtub Spring creates a flow that depends on the weather. In wet weather, you have to squish through soggy ground; in dry years, you will see only a trickle. At mile 4, the trail ends at the Crest Trail. Return the way you came.

MILLER CANYON TRAIL

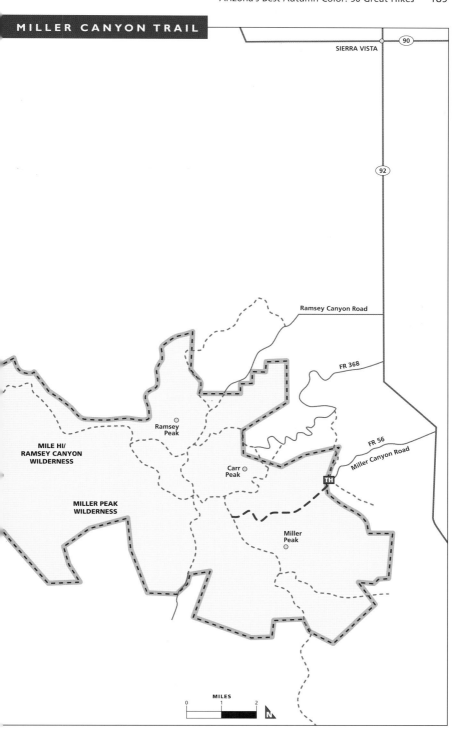

SIERRA VISTA

90

92

Ramsey Canyon Road

FR 368

Ramsey
Peak

FR 56

Miller Canyon Road

MILE HI/
RAMSEY CANYON
WILDERNESS

Carr
Peak

TH

MILLER PEAK
WILDERNESS

Miller
Peak

MILES

0   1   2

N

South Fork Trail

TRAIL RATING	easy to moderate
TRAIL LENGTH	3.5–6.8 miles one way
LOCATION	Chiricahua Mountains
ELEVATION	5,270–6,100 feet
CONTACT	Coronado National Forest, 520-364-3468
PEAK COLOR	end of October
SPECIAL CONSIDERATIONS	A $3 user fee per car is required.
DIRECTIONS	From Portal, drive west on FR 42 to FR 42E (South Fork of Cave Creek Road); drive 1.3 miles to the trailhead.

As one of several sky islands in southeastern Arizona, the Chiricahua Mountains have an unusual mix of flora and fauna. The mountains— a crossroads for plants and animals from the Rocky Mountains, the Sierra Madres, the Chiricahuan desert, and the Sonoran desert—attract plants and animals living on the fringes of their natural environments.

The mountains also have some exquisite geological formations. Wildly eroded rhyolite cliffs tumble steeply into oasislike canyons flowing with crystal water. The mountaintops have covers of mixed conifers and **aspen**, while the slopes display high desert vegetation. The canyons provide prime environments for **bigtooth maple** trees.

The South Fork Trail showcases all the chief characteristics of the mountain range, from diverse vegetation to stunning geology to incredible fall color. The trail starts in a cozy corridor of mixed oaks growing between the raspy rhyolite walls of the cavernous Cave Creek canyon system. This is known as a world-class birding area, so you may catch glimpses of some unusual birds while eyeing the fall colors.

Among golden **Gambel oak** leaves, you'll see drapes of **canyon grape** and prolific colonies of **poison ivy** that add yellow and red hues. **Arizona sycamore** trees rattle tan leaves from argentine trunks.

Within 0.5 mile, the canyon cliffs start to rise and squeeze in on the trail. That's when you'll notice the first show of **bigtooth maple** trees, also fittingly called **canyon maple**, adding a burst of color against buff boulders.

On a cloudless day, their crimson leaves are a stunning contrast against a cyan sky. Just past an S-gate, look for the flame of **Virginia creeper**.

Beyond Maple Camp at mile 1.5, the color only gets better as the trail sticks closely to the creek where the **bigtooth maple** trees thrive, crossing back and forth over its rocky bed. By mile 2, the trail passes through some exquisite shows of color. After mile 2.5, the trail starts to climb up the canyon walls, too far above the creek for the **bigtooth maple** trees to follow. Still, at mile 3.5, you see their color glowing in a panoramic view encompassing the whole canyon and the unique formations eroded in the canyon walls. This is the best turnaround point.

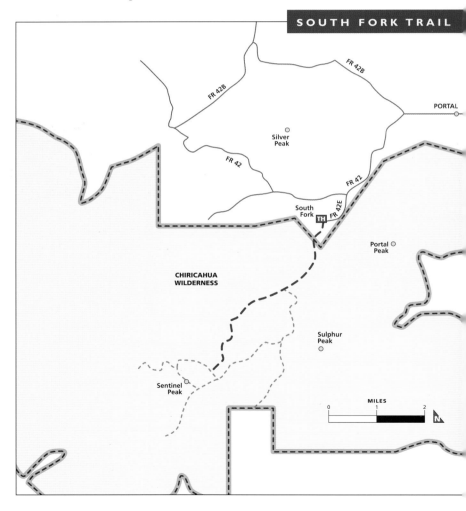

The trail flirts with the fall color as it runs up and down the canyon walls, crossing back and forth over the creek. By mile 5, the trail gets dicey with fallen logs and washouts. A good dose of adventure helps you negotiate some spots and good route-finding skills become more in demand from this point to the end of the trail.

POISON IVY
Rhus radicans

Attracted to disturbed areas, poison ivy often appears at the edges of trails passing through moist and shady environments. During the fall, their leaves acquire beautiful yellow and red hues. However, a poisonous resin called urushiol makes the plant the bane of the hiker's existence.

Though some people are more sensitive than others, most will experience a reaction when their skin is exposed to the plant. Often, people have no sensitivity to the plant on their first encounter with it, but become more sensitive with each subsequent experience. The affected area starts to itch within several hours, a rash appears, and eventually it oozes. The whole ordeal ends within one to four weeks.

Every part of the plant can cause an allergic reaction, from its leaves to its yellowish berries, whether the plant is verdant green or wearing its colorful fall frock. Even inhaling smoke from the plant will cause a rash.

If you brush up against the plant, immediately douse the area with cold water and wash with soap if possible. But the best remedy is prevention—leaves of three, let it be.

APPENDIX A: *Hikes by Difficulty*

The hikes in this book are all day hikes, and many trails are rated as easy or moderate. You can skim this list to find trails in your area that are suited to your hiking ability. Please note these are subjective ratings—one person's leisurely hike may be another's marathon trek. Check elevation ranges, trail lengths, and the descriptions for particular hikes to help you gauge the effort required. If you're a novice hiker, you may want to start out with itineraries described as having well-marked trails with little grade. But if you're an experienced hiker seeking adventure, look to the difficult hikes that feature rock hopping and steep descents into canyons. You may like to try a few to assess your own level; most of all, enjoy the experience!

Easy Hikes

Central Arizona
13. Hospital Canyon
14. West Fork Trail
17. Huckaby Trail
19. Crescent Moon Trail
23. Verde River Greenway

Southeastern Arizona
43. Bluff Loop
46. San Pedro Trail (easy to difficult)
50. South Fork Trail (easy to moderate)

Moderate Hikes

Northern Arizona
1. North Kaibab Plateau: Arizona Trail
2. Fence Point: Rainbow Rim Trail
3. North Timp Point: Rainbow Rim Trail
7. Bixler Saddle Trail
9. Inner Basin Trail
10. Kachina Trail

Central Arizona
16. Secret Canyon Trail
18. Bear Sign Trail
20. Parsons Trail
24. Bell Trail
27. Horton Creek Loop
29. Pine Mountain Loop
30. Cave Creek Trail

Eastern Arizona
33. Bonita Creek
38. White House Trail

Southeastern Arizona
39. Aravaipa Canyon
40. Marshall Gulch–Aspen Trail
47. Ramsey Canyon Trail
48. Scheelite Canyon Trail
     (moderate to strenuous)

Strenuous Hikes

Northern Arizona
4. North Kaibab Trail
5. Bill Williams Trail
6. Benham Trail

Central Arizona
15. Sterling Pass Trail
21. North Mingus Trail
22. View Point Trail
25. Fossil Creek Trail
26. Pine Canyon Trail
32. Six Shooter Trail

Eastern Arizona
34. Bear Wallow Loop
35. Escudilla National Recreation Trail
36. KP Creek Trail
37. Lanphier Trail

Southeastern Arizona
41. Butterfly Trail
42. Sycamore Reservoir Trail
44. Ash Creek Trail
45. Arcadia and Heliograph Trails
49. Miller Canyon Trail

Difficult Hikes

Northern Arizona
8. Abineau–Bear Jaw Loop
11. Weatherford Trail
12. Pumphouse Wash

Central Arizona
28. See Canyon Trail
31. Fish Creek Canyon

APPENDIX B: *Bibliography*

Angier, Bradford. *Field Guide to Medicinal Wild Plants.* Harrisburg, Pa.: Stackpole Books, 1978.

Brown, Tom, Jr. *Tom Brown's Guide to Wild Edible and Medicinal Plants.* New York: Berkley Books, 1985.

Duke, James A. *The Green Pharmacy.* Emmaus, Pa.: Rodale Press, 1997.

Elmore, Francis H. *Shrubs and Trees of the Southwest Uplands.* Tucson: Southwest Parks and Monuments Association, 1976.

Epple, Anne Orth. *A Field Guide to the Plants of Arizona.* Helena, Mont.: Falcon Press, 1995.

Granger, Byrd Howell. *Arizona Names: X Marks the Place.* Tucson: Falconer Publishing Co., 1983.

Lust, John. *The Herb Book.* Simi Valley, Calif.: Benedict Lust Publications, 1974.

Mayes, Vernon O., and Barbara Bayless Lacy. *Nanise': A Navajo Herbal.* Tsaile, Ariz.: Navajo Community College Press, 1990.

Palmer, Maggie, and George Palmer. *Western Trees: A Field Guide.* Helena, Mont.: Falcon Press, 1998.

Tweit, Susan J. *The Great Southwest Nature Fact Book.* Seattle: Alaska Northwest Books, 1992.

———. *Meet the Wild Southwest.* Seattle: Alaska Northwest Books, 1995.

Index

Steve Bruno

Christine Maxa

Christine, an award-winning freelance writer, has written for
*Arizona Highways, National Geographic Traveler, Backpacker
Magazine,* and *Midwest Express Magazine,* among other national
and regional publications, and she has been featured on a radio
show. She wrote the "Hike of the Week" column for the daily
Arizona Republic for more than two years and is the executive
assistant on the Advisory Committee for the Arizona State
Committee on Trails.